ABRAHAM LINCOLN
AND
AMERICAN POLITICAL RELIGION

ABRAHAM LINCOLN

AND

AMERICAN POLITICAL RELIGION

Glen E. Thurow

State University of New York Press
Albany, New York, 1976

First Edition

Published by
State University of New York Press
99 Washington Avenue, Albany, New York 12210

© 1976 State University of New York
All rights reserved.

Printed in the United States of America

Library of Congress Cataloging in Publication Data

Thurow, Glen E.
Abraham Lincoln and American political religion.

Includes bibliographical references.
1. Lincoln, Abraham, Pres. U. S., 1809-1865—Religion.
I. Title.
E457.2.T44   320.5'092'4   76-12596
ISBN 0-87395-334-7

CONTENTS

Acknowledgements. vii

Preface. ix

   I.   Introduction: Religion and Politics. 1

   II. Reverence for the Laws. 20

   III. Equality and Justice. 38

   IV. The Gettysburg Address and Sacred Politics. 63

   V. The Second Inaugural and the Limits of Politics. . . . 88

   VI. Conclusion: Transcending Politics. 109

Notes. 120

Selected Bibliography. 127

Index. 130

ACKNOWLEDGEMENTS

I am indebted, above all, to Professor Harvey C. Mansfield, Jr. of Harvard University who guided the production of the original of this book. One could not have asked for more gentle nor more incisive guidance. How does one express his debt to a true teacher? This book would not exist without the encouragement and assistance of Professor Richard Cox of the State University of New York at Buffalo. A friend and former colleague, he has shown me in deed the meaning of those words.

PREFACE

Several generations have passed since Woodrow Wilson wrote in 1885 that

> . . . we of the present generation are in the first season of free, outspoken, unrestrained constitutional criticism. We are the first Americans to hear our own countrymen ask whether the Constitution is still adapted to serve the purposes for which it was intended. . . .

An "undiscriminating and almost blind worship" of the Constitution had begun almost immediately after its adoption and continued until the Civil War. Even then, ". . . the most violent policies took care to make show of at least formal deference to the worshipful fundamental law." Almost all Americans were unshakably convinced that our institutions were the best in the world.

Wilson thought that the homage that had been rendered the Constitution was both good and bad. "Anyone," he said, "can see the reasons for it and the benefits of it without going far out of his way. . . ." But neither the reasons nor the benefits detained him. Inspired by the conviction that such homage was unworthy of free men, Wilson proudly noted that men had freed themselves of this unquestioning obeisance. Men could now freely consider the possibility that their institutions might be inferior to those of Europe and could think of remodeling the Constitution itself. Men could bravely face the facts of their political life freed from the spell of the Founders' "theories".[1]

Wilson's call for unfettered criticism has been heeded. Now, more than ninety years later, the critical spirit has reached almost to the lowest citizen. In its progress through the Progressive historians and their descendants (both within and without the profession of history), this spirit has turned from criticizing to debunking men and institutions previously hallowed.[2] So triumphant has been its march that today one must go to the backwoods to discover a college freshman who does not believe some variant of the Beardian thesis that the Founders were wealthy men who created the Constitution to thwart democracy and aid the interests of their class. Yet it is now widely recognized that we have not gained the unclouded sight and better institutions Wilson sought in giving up those nameless benefits he thought obvious. While our fundamental institutions are no longer shielded from criticism, they are as effectively as ever shielded from clear-eyed examination. Worship does not breed inquiry, but neither does contempt.

Nowhere is this more evident than in the study of the speeches and writings of statesmen. Traditionally it was held that to understand a statesman one had above all to understand his public statements. The height of Jefferson's statescraft could be seen in the Declaration of Independence; Washington's magnanimity and prudence viewed in his Farewell Address; Madison's architectonic calculations recognized in the *Federalist Papers*. The newer view held that a stateman's words were but a rationalization for his actions, or a screen behind which he could carry out deeds he could not defend in public. Speech was thought a weapon in a battle whose ends and true purposes must be found in psychology, the forces of history, economic interest, or other factors either not recognized or not acknowledged by the statesman himself.

The effect of this view of men's words was that the statesmen of former times literally disappeared as statesmen. Not only were there no heroes because all men were presumed to be creatures of forces they did not know and could not control, but one could not even see the character of the actions that took place. Statesmanship is the capacity to accomplish the public good.[3] A statesman is to be recognized not only by his ability to reach his ends, but by his judgment of what the public good requires. Yet what constitutes the public good is debatable and deeply problematical, involving many of the most perplexing questions of human life. When one recognizes this fact, one sees that one must know not only what a statesman did but why he did it to understand his action. For he may have had a view of the public good not only radically different from ours, but it may even be a view that would put our own view in doubt if we understood it. One cannot understand the American revolutionaries, for example, without understanding their view (expressed in the Declaration of Independence) of when it is just to declare oneself independent. Furthermore it is difficult to understand even the forces with which a statesman worked without seeing his estimate of them. In fact forces may be forces precisely because they are opinions of powerful or numerous men. What a statesman says, of course, should not be naively accepted. One must look for lies or misunderstandings, and one must consider what is implied or left unsaid as well as what is explicitly stated. To judge a statesman one must look at more than his words, and check his words by his actions, but his words remain the best access we have to his understanding and his reasons for doing what he did)

There are now significant elements in both political science and history that have rejected the "debunker's" view of speech. The development of an opposing view has been led by Leo Strauss and his students in political science and by the "New England" school in history—Perry Miller, Bernard Bailyn, Gordon Wood, and others. Although these two groups of scholars have written in almost complete independence of one another, and although there are significant differences between them, they are agreed in believing that one must look to men's thoughts—to their speeches and writings—in order to understand their actions.[4] These men have opened again the study of statesmanship)

This work is a study of the thought of Abraham Lincoln as found in his speeches and writings. Its motivation is not unreflecting reverence for great men nor curiosity about historical contingencies, but concern with an aspect of the problem that was central to Lincoln's thought: the capacity of a people to govern themselves. Lincoln's thought is not looked upon as a cover for, or rationalization of, his other deeds. Nor is it measured by its influence on subsequent generations, though Lincoln's great influence is not denied, and provides a motive for interest in Lincoln. Rather this study aims to examine Lincoln's opinions and the reasoning supporting them, explicit and implicit. It does not seek to debunk because it regards Lincoln's thought as sufficiently good to merit serious examination; it cannot worship because it seeks to understand. Its author's view is that the deepest grounds for both praise and criticism of Lincoln are to be found through his speeches and writings.)

Political Religion

(The problem of this book is the problem of political religion as it appears in Abraham Lincoln. The questions of whether Lincoln had a private faith in God and, if so, what his beliefs were, are unanswerable. Although these questions have stirred many men, both scholars and non-scholars, since Lincoln's law partner, William Herndon, tendentiously announced that the dead Lincoln had been an unbeliever, we have no reliable knowledge of Lincoln's private faith, if there was any. We have only the testimony of men like Herndon who heard what they wished to hear. Our only trustworthy knowledge of Lincoln's "religion" appears in his public speeches and writings. These works reveal that Lincoln's thought was preoccupied with politics, to say the least. Except for a few expressions of sympathy, from which little can be deduced, all of Lincoln's religious expressions appear as part of utterances that directly address political problems, that are given in a political context, or that intend to have political effects. Lincoln's religion, as we know it, is part of his political rhetoric and cannot be divorced from it. In this sense, at least, Lincoln's religion is political religion.

Let me hasten to say that this is not to argue that Lincoln was insincere or that he simply sought to foster religious beliefs in order to support political institutions. Lincoln was indeed tactful in trying to enlist the aid of important religious groups for the Union side. Any prudent statesman would have done as much in mid-nineteenth century America. But this does not constitute the substance of his political religion. Religion, in Lincoln, cannot be understood as an opiate used to drug a people into insensate acceptance of that which could not be rationally defended. Rather, I shall argue that Lincoln's religion is the culmination of a reasoned reflection about American politics.

(I shall show that Lincoln's political religion was an attempt, on the one hand, to reconcile the claims of the universal principle of the Declaration of Independence, that all men are created equal, with the claims of the nation that the Declaration created; and, on the other, to reconcile the claims of the mass of the people and those of the extraordinary man. Lincoln saw that there were opposing dangers for the United States: either that people would forsake the principle of justice upon which the United States was founded and which made it worth preserving; or that the people, acting on principle, would become a fanatical, mob-like beast deaf to the voice of prudence. His political religion is an attempt to steer the United States between this Scylla and Charybdis. The problem that Lincoln faced, as well as the solution he crafted, remains with us today and calls for no less thought than it did a century ago.)

I.
INTRODUCTION
RELIGION AND POLITICS

"Political religion" seems to combine two things that ought to be separated—politics and religion. On the one hand it suggests the danger that politics will be inflamed with passions of religious intensity or made subservient to the designs of a clergy claiming special dispensation. On the other, it offers the specter of religion debased by the arts of wordly politics or threatened by the irreligion of partisan politicians. A proper concern both for men's salvation and for their political liberty and peace seems to demand that a "wall of separation" be erected between politics and religion.

Indeed, this opinion seems to be enshrined in the American Constitution. The First Amendment to the Constitution provides that "Congress shall make no law respecting an establishment of religion, or prohibiting the free exercise thereof . . . ," thus guaranteeing that no religion shall have a position of national authority from which it may claim the power of the state to impose its own ends, and also assuring that men may have the liberty to worship as they please without the danger of political corruption.

This dual concern of the Constitution is also found in the political philosophy of liberalism, as espoused by John Locke:

> But, however, that some may not colour their spirit of persecution and unchristian cruelty with a pretence of care of the public weal and observation of the laws; and others, under pretence of religion, may not seek impunity for their libertinism and licentiousness; in a word, that none may impose either upon himself or others, by the pretences of loyalty and obedience to the prince, or of tenderness and sincerity in the worship of God; I esteem it above all things necessary to distinguish exactly the

1

business of civil government from that of religion, and to settle the just bounds that lie between the one and the other.[2]

That we are a liberal democracy, not a pure democracy, means, among other things, that politics is free of ecclesiastical authority and religion free of political authority.)

It perhaps does not come as much of a surprise that the United States has never seen the complete separation of politics and religion. Not only is there vast governmental encouragement of religion through indirect means—one need only be reminded of the tremendous advantage given religion through tax-exemption—but there is also much direct governmental encouragement. Nearly all of the most solemn state papers and speeches in American history have referred to God. Every Presidential inaugural address, with the exception of the perfunctory Second Inaugural of Washington, has referred to God. The motto, "In God We Trust," found on our coins, and the pledge to the flag, ("...one nation, under God..."), as well, perhaps, as such a national holiday as Thanksgiving give religion a conspicuous public place in our political life.[3]

Yet, for all their pervasiveness, these manifestations of religion by themselves do not necessarily raise any doubts about the wisdom of the separation of politics and religion. They may merely show that political ends cannot be arrived at by doctrinaire means. Some of them may be required or permitted by the Constitution in order to assure religious liberty (perhaps tax-exemption might be defended on this ground). Others may be necessary concessions to the religious sensibilities of the people, but in no substantial way aid or inhibit religion or give the government religious ends (perhaps some of the references to religion in state papers are of this character). Or some may simply be violations of the Constitution that the courts or other branches of government have not yet got around to rooting out for one reason or another (as the Supreme Court decided prayers in schools were not so long ago).)

What demands closer attention is that many of the greatest American statesmen have thought that the kind of government the Constitution erected involved a connection between politics and religion. Among the Founders even those who were most adamant that the new government required separation of church and state thought that politics required religion. Thomas Jefferson, more than any other man, has been given credit for establishing religious liberty in the American government. Unlike many of the signers of the Declaration of Independence, Jefferson thought one of its central purposes was to free men from "monkish ignorance and superstition." He regarded his "Bill for Establishing Religious Freedom" in Virginia one of the three most notable works of his life, and rejected most of the traditional theological doctrines of Christianity.[4] Yet in discussing the threat to liberty posed by slavery (in his *Notes on the State of Virginia*), Jefferson cites its threat to religious belief:

> And can the liberties of a nation be thought secure when we have removed their only firm basis, a conviction in the minds of the people that these liberties are of the gift of God? That they are not to be violated but with his wrath? Indeed I tremble for my country when I reflect that God is just; that his justice cannot sleep forever; that considering numbers, nature and natural means only, a revolution of the wheel of fortune, an exchange of situation is among possible events; that it may become probable by supernatural interference! The Almighty has no attribute which can take side with us in such a contest.[5]

In the face of the mighty passions aroused by slavery, men's liberties need the support they find in the conviction that these liberties are from God. While the state cannot establish religion nor use its laws to enforce belief or worship, the state apparently can use the means of persuasion at its disposal to help establish this conviction—as Jefferson taught that "nature's God" entitled Americans to independence in the Declaration of Independence.

Perhaps the most impressive statements about the connection between religion and politics made by the Founders are to be found in George Washington. In his "Farewell Address" (which had been written with the collaboration of Hamilton and Madison), he said:

> Of all the dispositions and habits which lead to political prosperity, religion and morality are indispensable supports. In vain would that man claim the tribute of patriotism who should labor to subvert these great pillars of human happiness, these firmest props of the duties of men and citizens. The mere politician, equally with the pious man, ought to respect and to cherish

them. . . . let us with caution indulge the supposition that morality can be maintained without religion. Whatever may be conceded to the influence of refined education on minds of peculiar structure, reason and experience both forbid us to expect that national morality can prevail in exclusion of religious principle.[6]

Washington, like Jefferson, not only invokes God, but also argues that politics needs religion. Both men's opinions show that the direct and indirect governmental encouragement of religion may be based, at least in part, upon an argument that certain religious beliefs are beneficial to American politics and may properly be encouraged by government)

The Supreme Court and Separation of Church and State

Now the nature of this argument and the issues it involves are largely forgotten in contemporary political discussion of the relationship of church and state. The issues raised have been regarded as questions of private rights, or of the extent of public accomodation of private desires and needs, rather than issues directly involving the common public good. This can be seen by examining one of these recent disputes. Perhaps the most controversial area in church-state relations since World War II has been education. Two practical questions have been raised: To what extent should government aid to schools be available to parochial schools or parochial school children? and, To what extent should religious activities and instruction be permitted in the public schools?)

These questions have been raised as Constitutional issues. To see the underlying issue in dispute and the understanding the Supreme Court has of it, we may look at two relatively early cases in the history of recent litigation, *Zorach v. Clauson*, and *Abington School District v. Schempp*.[7] In the first case a released time program for religious instruction was declared constitutional. In the second, a requirement for Bible reading in the public schools was declared unconstitutional)

Zorach v. Clauson and a Religious People

In *Zorach v. Clauson* the 1952 Court held a New York City program under which pupils were excused from school to attend religious instruction and devotional exercises to be constitutional, unlike a somewhat similar program in Illinois declared unconstitutional in *McCollum v. Board of Education.*[8] Justice Douglas, speaking for the Court in the case, argued that no coercion was involved in releasing the pupils from school for religious instruction and hence that there was no infringement of the free exercise of religion. He went on to argue that while the separation of church and state must be complete in that there could be no interference with the free exercise of religion nor any establishment of religion, there need not be separation in all respects. To declare the program unconstitutional, the Court would have to declare any connection whatever between church and state, even the Court's own opening words at each session ("God save the United States and this Honorable Court"), to be unconstitutional. Not only would this be carrying the notion of separation of church and state to ridiculous extremes, but, he maintained:

> We are a religious people whose institutions presuppose a Supreme Being. We guarantee the freedom to worship as one chooses. We make room for as wide a variety of beliefs and creeds as the spiritual needs of man deem necessary. We sponsor an attitude on the part of government that shows no partiality to any one group and lets each flourish according to the zeal of its adherents and the appeal of its dogma. When the state encourages religious instruction or cooperates with religious authorities by adjusting the schedule of public events to sectarian needs, it follows the best of our traditions. For it then respects the religious nature of our people and accomodates the public service to their spiritual needs. To hold that it may not would be to find in the Constitution a requirement that the government show a callous indifference to religious groups. That would be preferring those who believe in no religion over those who do believe.[9]

Let us look closely at the elements of this remarkable statement. The main assertion, contained in the first sentence, is that we are a religious people whose institutions presuppose a Supreme Being. If this be so, then the policy of freedom of religion as described in the next three sentences must not be interpreted as resulting from the fact that the state is indifferent to this relationship. If our institutions do in fact depend upon a Supreme Being, then those charged with defending these institutions surely could not be indifferent to that dependency. The statement's inclusion in an opinion of the Court is testimony that the dependency has practical consequences. Rather the policy of freedom of religion is justified as the policy most conducive to creating an appropriate recognition of the relationship between our institutions and a Supreme Being. The clearest expression in this passage of why Justice Douglas considers the policy of freedom of religion to be an appropriate recognition of dependency is the claim that men's spiritual needs make necessary a wide variety of beliefs and creeds, and that the way to achieve such beneficial variety is for the government to show no partiality, letting each group flourish as best it can amid the competition of other groups.

The Court then argues that the released time program is not only constitutional, but follows the best of our traditions because it respects the religious nature of our people and accomodates their spiritual needs. Respecting the religious nature of our people might be interpreted as a counsel of expediency made necessary because of the outcry that would attend the alternative. But if it is, the argument in any case goes beyond expediency when it suggests that men have spiritual needs. The state ought to accommodate sectarian activities not only because of expediency but because there are spiritual needs which it is good to meet, and which are met through sectarian activities. Finally Justice Douglas argues that if the state were to find such recognition and accommodation unconstitutional, the ruling would indicate "callous" indifference towards religion, and would be preferring those who do not believe over those who do. We will investigate the possible grounds for this assertion below. Douglas's contentions in the case may be summarized: 1) Our people are religious and have spiritual needs, and our institutions presuppose a Supreme Being, 2) A suitable way of acknowledging these facts is comprised by the policy known as freedom of religion, which encourages a beneficial variety of sects and shows no partiality to any, 3) This policy must not be carried to the point where freedom becomes confused with callous indifference or, in other words, to the point where the state no longer recognizes the dependency of our institutions on a Supreme Being or the religious needs of our people. Our Constitution, the Court implies, favors no sect, encourages many sects, and prefers this non-exclusive religion over irreligion. But why our political order requires such a policy is not evident in the opinion of the Court. The connection between men's "spiritual needs" and the dependency of our political institutions upon a Supreme Being is not clear. In fact even the meaning of these statements is uncertain.)

Abington and a Praying People

It is not surprising, therefore, that one finds a different position in the *Abington* case. In *Abington* the 1963 Court ruled that a requirement of Pennsylvania law that ten verses of the Bible be read each day in school was unconstitutional because it violated the establishment clause of the First Amendment, as included in the Fourteenth.)

The difference in interpretation is apparent from the beginning of the opinion although the Court attempts to show that its opinion is consistent with all previous cases concerning the establishment clause. Justice Clark for the Court cites the first sentence of Douglas's statement quoted above and a statement from *Engel v. Vitale* that "The history of man is inseparable from the history of religion."[10] He then notes that many of the Founding Fathers believed in God, cites numerous contemporary practices in which the state recognizes religion, and concludes:

> It can be truly said therefore, that today, as in the beginning, our national life reflects a religious people who, in the words of Madison, are "earnestly praying, as . . . in duty bound, that the Supreme Lawgiver of the Universe . . . guide them into every measure which may be worthy of his [blessing . . .].[11])

If one compares this statement to that quoted from the *Zorach* case, a subtle shift can be discerned. What is left out is more important than what is said: The Court does not contend that our institutions presuppose a Supreme Being, or that men have spiritual needs, but only that our people are religious in that they are praying. All that is recognized is that our people do in fact participate in religious observances; there is no recognition by the Court of any spiritual needs of the people or any dependence of our institutions on a Divine Being. The Court does not say whether it is good or bad that our national life reflects a religious people.)

The religious practices and expressions cited by the Court are designated as one of our traditions. Justice Clark then opposes to them, as another tradition of ours, the policy of freedom of religion: "This is not to say, however, that religion has been so identified with our history and government that religious freedom is not likewise as strongly imbedded in our public and private life."[12] The implied interpretation of *Zorach* that this policy is a means of recognizing the fact that our people have spiritual needs and that our institutions presuppose a Supreme Being is implicitly denied. Rather this policy is interpreted as a separate, if not opposing, tradition to that represented by our religious practices. Religion and the policy of freedom of religion are no longer seen as having a common root in recognition of presumed spiritual needs and in-stitutional dependency on a Supreme Being. There is not one tradition, but two.)

This interpretation is maintained with more or less consistency throughout the opinion. When discussing the free exercise clause, the Court seems to judge that it is founded on a belief in the value of religious training and observance,[13] but it is precisely this judg-ment that the Court refuses to make when discussing the establish-ment clause.[14] After reviewing the history of the Court's rulings concerning the First Amendment clauses, the Court comes to a conclusion as to the meaning of the clauses which it states at the end of the opinion: "In the relationship between man and religion, the State is firmly committed to a position of neutrality."[15] Applying this general rule to legislative enactments gives the following test: ". . . what are the purpose and primary effect of the enactment? If either is the advancement or inhibition of religion then the enact-ment exceeds the scope of legislative power as circumscribed by the Constitution."[16] An important point to note is that the Court does not mean by religion simply institutionalized religion. Rather it means to cover all questions concerned with religion including the possible recognition of a dependency of our institutions upon a Supreme Being. In framing its ordinances, the state must not rec-ognize any good or evil in religion any more than it can aid any religious group. The policy of separation of church and state is not regarded as an appropriate way to recognize the spiritual needs of men, but reflects the fact that any such spiritual needs are a matter in which the state need take, and should take, no concern. The spiritual needs of men as met by religion, if there are any, are unimportant to the state and need not be recognized in its calculations. The neutrality of the state extends not only to particular religions and sects, but also to any question regarding God or the spiritual needs of men)

The Court, in saying that the state is indifferent to the question of religion or irreligion, is saying that secularism is sufficient for our political order, for it does not matter if secularism should win out through neglect of religion. The Court seems to be saying that our Constitution requires either religion which does not claim the right to rule or no religion at all—and that it does not matter which)

Justice Stewart in dissent denies that the Court's decision reflects the principle of governmental neutrality. He argues that the opinion establishes opposition to religion, not merely neutrality. If one denies a community the right to read the Bible in the schools even if no coercion is involved, is he not restricting the free exercise of religion? The Justice argues that the school so structures a child's day that to deny a school the power to have the Bible read is in effect to establish a religion of secularism:

> And a refusal to permit religious exercises thus is seen, not as the realization of state neutrality, but rather as the establishment of a religion of secularism, or at the least, as government support of the beliefs of those who think that religious exercises shall be conducted only in private.[17]

Justices Goldberg and Harlan, while concurring in the decision of the Court, raise the same issue concerning the reasoning of the Court's opinion:

> But unilateral devotion to the concept of neutrality can lead to invocation or approval of results which partake not simply of that noninterference and noninvolvement with the religious which the Constitution commands, but of a brooding and pervasive devotion to the secular and a passive, or even active, hostility to the religious.[18]

Stewart, Harlan, and Goldberg thus interpret the opinion of the Court as reflecting hostility to religion, not neutrality.

It is not necessary, however, to agree with the dissenting and concurring arguments in order to see the difference of principle between *Zorach* and *Abington*. The first says that separation of church and state as embodied in the First Amendment means that the government must treat religion in such a way that no sect is favored at the expense of another, and that no sect may rule, but that it is permissable to favor non-sectarian religion over secularism. The other opinion says that the state must be neutral not only between sects, but also between non-sectarian religion and secularism. Whether the Court further says that in case of irreconcilable conflict one must prefer secularism is debatable. To simplify the opinions of the cases, the conflict is whether the country may be permitted or even encouraged to become secular or whether our political institutions require a non-sectarian and tolerant, but still religious, opinion. Yet the cases do not reveal the grounds for these differing opinions.

Although the Zorach and Abington cases differ in their conclusions and in their contentions about the place of religion in American life, they agree in how the issue should be framed. Both agree that the problem is one of the degree of accommodation to be accorded private religious desires and practices. Justice Douglas asserts that our institutions presuppose a Supreme Being, but he discusses only the accommodation of private desires and needs. Neither opinion raises directly the question of the public good involved. As under the theory of *laissez faire* in economics, the theory of the Court is that it is the function of government to allow or facilitate and to harmonize the private religious or irreligious desires of individual citizens, without any explicit consideration of the public good. But we may wonder whether the conflicting private desires of citizens can be harmonized for the public good without considering what the public good as a whole requires. Indeed, as we have seen, each case has an implied but undefended view of the public good.

Abraham Lincoln and Political Religion

The speeches of Abraham Lincoln have been held to be the best expression of our democracy. It is equally true that Lincoln is the central figure of American political religion. This is not only because of the way in which Americans have venerated him; it is chiefly because of what Lincoln himself said.[19] Both the Gettysburg Address and the Second Inaugural, Lincoln's two most famous speeches, make clear his importance. Lord Charnwood, the biographer who has most revealed Lincoln's character, commented on the Second Inaugural: "Probably no other speech of a modern statesman uses so unreservedly the language of intense religious feeling."[20] Said Lincoln:

> The Almighty has His own purposes. "Woe unto the world because of offences! for it must needs be that offences come; but woe to that man by whom the offence cometh!" If we shall suppose that American Slavery is one of those offences which, in the providence of God, must needs come, but which, having continued through His appointed time, He now wills to remove, and that He gives to both North and South, this terrible war, as the woe due to those by whom the offence came, shall we discern therein any departure from those divine attributes which the believers in a Living God always ascribe to Him! Fondly do we hope—fervently do we pray—that this mighty scourge of war may speedily pass away. Yet, if God wills that it continue, until all the wealth piled up by the bond-man's two hundred and fifty years of unrequited toil shall be sunk, and until every drop of blood drawn with the lash, shall be paid by another drawn with the sword, as was said three thousand years ago, so still it must be said, "the judgements of the Lord, are true and righteous altogether."[21]

The language of the Gettysburg Address, on the other hand, is not so explicitly theological. Apart from the phrase "under God" (which could be merely perfunctory), the speech contains nothing explicitly religious. Yet religion seems somehow evoked. The Biblical cadences of the language, the theme of birth, death, and rebirth, the overtones in the dedication of the nation to equality that suggest the dedication of a child to God in baptism, and in the testing of that nation that suggest the test of religious faith; all endow the speech with the seriousness and solemnity of religion. The Second Inaugural sees the nation under the providence and judgment of God; the Gettysburg Address appropriates for the nation the language and the dignity of religion.

A host of books were written in the late nineteenth and early twentieth centuries seeking to show that Lincoln was a conventional believer of one sort or another. But the beauty and power of Lincoln's words must make us wonder whether they do not reflect an understanding equally beautiful and powerful. Lord Charnwood again catches the problem in speaking of the Second Inaugural:

> ... neither the thought nor the words are in any way conventional; no sensible reader now could entertain a suspicion that the orator spoke to the heart of the people but did not speak from his own heart. But an old Illinois attorney, who thought he knew the real Lincoln behind the President, might have wondered whether the real Lincoln spoke here.[22]

The old Illinois attorney to whom Charnwood refers was Lincoln's law partner, William H. Herndon, who, with other of Lincoln's close associates, claimed after his death that Lincoln was not a believer in Christianity; some even testified that he was an atheist. Herndon tells us that as a young man Lincoln was a skeptic and associated with fellow skeptics in New Salem. In 1834 he supposedly wrote an essay showing that the Bible was not God's inspired word nor Jesus God's divine son. An employer, either scandalized or fearing its effects on Lincoln's future, threw it into the stove. Lincoln's first law partner told Herndon that Lincoln was "an avowed and open infidel, and sometimes bordered on atheism."[23] Herndon did not believe that Lincoln's skeptical opinions ever changed. As he put it:

> Lincoln was very politic, and a very shrewd man in some particulars. When he was talking to a Christian, he adapted himself to the Christian ... he was at moments, as it were, a Christian, through politeness, courtesy, or good breeding toward the delicate, tender-nerved man, the Christian, and in two minutes after, in the absence of such men, and among his own kind, the same old unbeliever.[24]

Lincoln never belonged to a church, although he sometimes attended with his wife.

Various explanations have been given for the apparent dichotomy between the private and the public Lincoln, beginning with Herndon's explanation that Lincoln merely used conventional religious language because he was president of a religious people. A reading of the Second Inaugural and Gettysburg Address should convince one, however, that this explanation is hardly sufficient.[25]

For it is not so much the fact that Lincoln refers to God that requires attention as it is the character of his references. One need only compare the Second Inaugural with the invocations of God that have graced almost every inaugural address. Typical is Franklin Roosevelt's First Inaugural, at the end of which he says, "In this dedication of a Nation we humbly ask the blessing of God. May He protect each and every one of us. May He guide me in the days to come."[26] Perhaps the most impressive supplication, other than Lincoln's, is found in Washington's First Inaugural Address:

> . . . it would be peculiarly improper to omit in this first official act my fervent supplications to that Almighty Being who rules over the universe, who presides in the councils of nations, and whose providential aids can supply every human defect. . . . In tendering this homage to the Great Author of every public and private good, I assure myself that it expresses your sentiments not less than my own, nor those of my fellow-citizens at large less than either. No people can be bound to acknowledge and adore the invisible Hand which conducts the affairs of men more than those of the United States. . . . These reflections, arising out of the present crisis, have forced themselves too strongly on my mind to be suppressed. You will join with me, I trust, in thinking that there are none under the influence of which the proceedings of a new and free government can more auspiciously commence.[27]

It would seem that a man who was chiefly concerned about wounding men's sensibilities might rather speak as Washington did than as Lincoln did. For Washington tenders a general thanks to the Almighty, while directing men's thoughts to what is proper and what will find general assent. Lincoln sees the providence of God exacting punishment through war while directing men of the North as well as the South to their sins. As Lincoln said, such a message is not calculated to be immediately popular or to simply sooth men's prejudices. (This is not to say that Washington's words can be understood this way either.)

Whatever the relationship of Lincoln's words to conventional opinion, they cannot be understood simply as dictated by "politeness, courtesy, or good breeding." The other major explanation is that Lincoln experienced a conversion, or, since there does not seem to be one point at which Lincoln changed, several crises of the spirit.[28] This explanation gains some plausibility from the fact that the testimony regarding Lincoln's free-thinking comes mostly from his younger days. Herndon was not closely associated with Lincoln during his presidential years. However when one considers that the testimony about Lincoln's beliefs comes not only from his earlier career but from men, like Herndon, whose interests make their testimony suspect, one doubts the need for this explanation. Furthermore, evidence for the opinion is scanty, and largely rests upon presumed effects of years of personal misfortunes and heavy public burdens. What is not debatable, however, is what Lincoln himself said.

Lincoln did not merely echo the opinions of the day or give conventional acknowledgment to God. But it must be stressed that Lincoln's speeches were political speeches. Even before he became president, nearly all of his speeches were delivered on political occasions and with political purposes in mind. Insofar as religious expressions entered them, these expressions are entwined with and serve the political purposes of the speeches. The Second Inaugural, just quoted, was preeminently a political speech, dictated by long-established political custom, yet spoke of the relation of God to the nation. Religion is present in Lincoln's speeches because of its relevance to political problems. Much of the confusion surrounding Lincoln's religion stems from the fact that commentators have tried to see whether he belonged to the religion of the churches, neglecting the possibility that his speeches were political, not religious; or were religious because they were political. Lincoln leads us, not to religion, but to political religion. We do not look to Lincoln to find personal piety, but to find a carefully-thought-out understanding of political religion in America.

The Charge against Lincoln

To the extent that Lincoln's religious expressions have been considered in a political light, they have either been dismissed or condemned. In the former case their significance has been disregarded; in the latter their significance has been misunderstood. The point may be illustrated by considering two interpretations of the Second Inaugural Address.

One senses a slight embarrassment or charitable silence in some men who have been moved by the words of Lincoln's Second Inaugural. For example, Richard Current, in the last volume of Randall's *Lincoln the President*, concludes that it is the final paragraph that makes the speech forever memorable. Said Lincoln:

> With malice toward none; with charity for all, with firmness in the right, as God gives us to see the right, let us strive on to finish the work we are in; to bind up the nation's wounds; to care for him who shall have borne the battle, and for his widow, and his orphan—to do all which may achieve and cherish a just, and a lasting peace, among ourselves, and with all nations.[29]

Lincoln's magnanimity, counseling charity, is indeed memorable. Concerning the rest of the address, however, Current asks only, "Was Lincoln sincere?"[30] It is as if, when one had shown Lincoln to be sincere or insincere, he could then pass over in silence the substance of what was said. Current does not consider whether the charitable sentiments expressed in the concluding paragraph depend upon the theology of the earlier paragraphs.

The earlier paragraphs are characterized by their theological speculations, as we have indicated. Indeed, the central portion of the Second Inaugural contains an assertion about the purposes of God, an inquiry concerning His qualities and an affirmation that His judgments are just. Furthermore the speech contains three quotations from the Bible.[31] These quotations are not simply decorative or illustrative, but form an integral part of the structure and meaning of the speech. One is an argument for not condemning the South as impious; another indicates the relationship between God's purposes and men's; and the third affirms that God's judgments are just.

No one has called attention to the religious language of the address with more insistence than Edgar Lee Masters, one of Lincoln's severest critics. His harsh criticism reveals what more temperate historians hide. Masters, unlike Current, considers the magnanimity of the Second Inaugural's concluding paragraph to be hypocrisy. Lincoln counsels charity, but he does not order the guns to cease firing. In Master's opinion he could have stopped the war or prevented its outbreak; in fact, he did neither.[32] Behind a facade of charitable sentiment, Lincoln is responsible for the horrors of civil war. His rhetoric hides a cruelty to match that of Robespierre.

The cause of Lincoln's alleged cruelty (and of the corruption of American civilization which Masters sees displayed in the war) is "Hebraic-Puritan superstition." The presumed moral principles for which the war was waged are derived from this superstition. These moral principles however, are illusions. They lead to war, and war is not moral, but cruel. Rather than securing the safety and allowing the happiness of the people, these "moral principles" bring on the unspeakable miseries of war. Yet the men who send the armies to battle do not accept responsibility for these miseries. They attribute the sufferings of war to the Providence of God, denying the human responsibility that has caused and might alleviate them. They preach peace while bearing swords. Cruelty masked by hypocrisy is thus the moral essence of the "Hebraic-Puritan" heritage in America, and the Second Inaugural is an infamous example of this heritage. After years of brooding upon "Hebraic-Puritan" ideas, Lincoln in the Second Inaugural became fixed in "the black of sternest Puritanism. . . . Not Jonathan Edwards in his maddest Calvanism ever uttered words to equal those of Lincoln."[33]

Current does not agree with Masters' judgment that the theological speculations of the Second Inaugural corrupted Lincoln's moral life, but neither does he think that they were the source of Lincoln's sublime charity. He rather thinks them irrelevant. He praises the final paragraph without examining the rest of the speech. His silence shows his agreement with the judgment of Paul Angle, who writes (in discussing Herndon's view of Lincoln): "Only the subject of Lincoln's religion remains [to be discussed]. In the light of modern liberalism the controversy [about it] seems foolish."[34]

The controversy about Lincoln's religion seems foolish because modern liberalism reveals that religion and morality are independent. Not only may there be rare men who will fulfill their duties without these duties bearing any sense of religious obligation (as Washington implies in his "Farewell Address"), but the social morality of men in general may prevail without religious support.[35] The modern liberal is embarrassed for Lincoln not because he may have had certain religious beliefs, which is his right, but because he does not realize that they are irrelevant in a political address.

Masters disagrees with Current in believing that Lincoln's theology affected his politics; however, Masters' frank atheism points to the danger of ignoring the distinction between religion and politics. Men will treat their own opinions as if they were sanctified by God. Politics may then become inflamed because the partisan nature of most political quarrels will be ignored and all will refuse to compromise.)

It is no defense of Lincoln that he did not seek to impose his views through law, but only through the persuasion of speech. The words of his Second Inaugural serve a powerful rhetoric. Furthermore, the speech was given on a most solemn public occasion, in words destined to be hailed as a masterpiece, to be inscribed in a national shrine, and to be read by every school child—a destiny which Lincoln did not request but for which he cannot disclaim responsibility. In fact, although he did not think his speech immediately popular, he believed his speech would endure and wrote to Thurlow Weed shortly after the inauguration, "I expect the [Second Inaugural Address] to wear as well as—perhaps better than—anything I have produced."[36]

Current's sympathy for Lincoln leads him to drop the subject of Lincoln's religion but leaves us without understanding what Lincoln thought he was doing. Masters presents a charge, expressed in passionate language, that Lincoln's use of religion expressed the corruption of the moral basis of American society. But he, too, like Current (for different reasons) does not listen to the defense Lincoln might have made. It is our aim to present that defense.)

The Gettysburg Address and the Second Inaugural

We have already noted that the Gettysburg Address and the Second Inaugural are the two speeches of Lincoln in which religious language is most pervasive. But it will not be amiss to add a further word concerning the emphasis these two speeches will be given in the remainder of this book/

Each of these speeches was given on a ceremonial occasion—the one at the dedication of the Gettysburg Cemetery, the other at Lincoln's inauguration as President for his second term. In both cases the occasion was such that low or blatant partisanship could not have been excused. On the other hand, it would be naive not to recognize that a higher, more subtle kind of partisanship could and does appear in these speeches. The Gettysburg Address and the Second Inaugural were of their times and their times included certain political alignments. The Gettysburg Address counsels re-dedication to freedom and to the cause of the nation at a time when the North had had notable triumphs on the battlefield but many months of fighting yet remained. Lincoln was then in the midst of a fight to secure the emancipation of the slaves (which had been but partially accomplished and only by executive order) and to neutralize the Radical Republican opposition to his reelection. It is not to denigrate Lincoln to suggest that the stress he places on freedom in the speech, seeing the nation's cause as a human struggle for freedom and democracy, is related to his political situation.)Similarly, the Second Inaugural counsels persever-ence and charity at a time when the war was obviously near its end, but also at a time when Lincoln had won his reelection battle and when the chief work ahead was his controversial plan for reconstruction. If nothing more, Lincoln can be said to have tried to set a tone which would aid his political program. The appropriate exclusion of low partisanship did not preclude partisanship of any kind.)

Yet in order to understand these speeches, it is necessary to see that the emphasis and practical counsel of each rests upon an underlying view of the nation and its politics that was the result of Lincoln's lifelong reflections on American politics and was meant in some way to stand independent of the immediate circumstances. Indeed men have not only felt that he spoke to times far different from those of 1863 or 1865, but also that Lincoln intended these speeches to be part of his legacy to future generations.

In the Gettysburg Address, Lincoln says that, "The world will little note, nor long remember what we say here . . . ," thus depre-cating his speech in comparison with the deeds of the battlefield. Yet the Address, as has been often noted, presents a general view at odds with his prediction: the sacrifice of the dead would be in vain if it did not renew dedication to the proposition that all men are created equal. That meaning of their deeds can be conveyed only through words, and their deeds can achieve their end only by men remembering Lincoln's words or some words like his. In ad-dition, the Address is couched in terms applicable to new times and circumstances. The references to particulars—to this war and this battlefield (neither of which is named)—emphasize the more general struggle to make government of the people, by the people, for the people imperishable.)

In the case of the Second Inaugural, we have explicit testimony. As we have already noted, Lincoln wrote in reply to a compliment from Thurlow Weed, "I expect the latter [the Second Inaugural Address] to wear as well as — perhaps better than — any thing I have produced; but I believe it is not immediately popular." Hence it is in accordance with Lincoln's own intentions, either explicit or implied, to read these speeches not only in light of the immediate circumstances, but in different circumstances for their more general teaching. The Gettysburg Address and the Second Inaugural are not only the speeches in which political religion is most apparent and pervasive, but they also contain or point to Lincoln's most enduring reflections on American government.[37]

II.
REVERENCE FOR THE LAWS

Political speeches are not meant merely to enlighten the disinterested, but to help bring about some desired state of affairs. They are part of the actions statesmen take to achieve their goals. In the Gettysburg Address Lincoln indicates the end he seeks both explicitly and implicitly. The exhortation is explicit:

> . . . that from these honored dead we take increased devotion to that cause for which they gave the last full measure of devotion—that we here highly resolve that these dead shall not have died in vain—that this nation, under God, shall have a new birth of freedom—and that government of the people, by the people, for the people, shall not perish from the earth.[1]

The exhortation sums up and drives home the message of the speech as a whole: the particular struggle of these dead and this nation is a struggle of universal significance. In the speech Lincoln sees his own words as part of the Civil War (deprecating their contribution to the struggle in comparison with the sacrifice of those who fought on the battlefield). The Civil War in turn is a test of whether "this nation, or any nation so conceived and so dedicated, can long endure."

Now it is evident that the Civil War was a crucial test of whether this nation could long endure. It is less evident that the war tested whether "any nation so conceived and so dedicated" can long endure. It is possible, even plausible, that the war and its outcome were rooted in causes peculiar to the United States. The existence of slavery, the constitutional and legal situation, the economic strengths and weaknesses of each side—all seem peculiar to the United States. It might appear that the collapse of such a nation would show little about its possibility elsewhere. We must see why

Lincoln thought the war the outcome not of causes unique to the United States but of causes inherent in the very kind of nation the United States was—one conceived in liberty and dedicated to the proposition that all men are created equal. Its very conception and dedication must make its endurance problematical, in Lincoln's view.)

We have seen the reasons why the Gettysburg Address and the Second Inaugural are central to Lincoln's political religion. But these compact speeches express the distilled essence of Lincoln's thought in a form designed to pierce the heart rather than to directly approach the head. Their reasoning, which all can sense, can be drawn out by attention to Lincoln's more elaborated and discursive speeches. Part of the answer to the question why Lincoln thought that the war was of universal significance is to be found in his Lyceum Speech, delivered in 1838 before the Young Men's Lyceum of Springfield. The peroration of the speech shows that Lincoln agreed with the commonly held view that nature had given more to the United States than to any other country:

> We find ourselves in the peaceful possession, of the fairest portion of the earth, as regards extent of territory, fertility of soil, and salubrity of climate.[2]

The United States could be a test of a particular kind of nation because its natural situation was the most favorable that existed. Furthermore,

> We find ourselves under the government of a system of political institutions, conducing more essentially to the ends of civil and religious liberty, than any of which the history of former times tells us.

Not only is the country's natural inheritance the best, but its political inheritance is the best that there has ever been. The task, says Lincoln, is simply to transmit this inheritance "to the latest generation that fate shall permit the world to know." Neither the natural environment nor the political inheritance may be perfect, Lincoln implies, but the one is the best there is and the other the best one could reasonably expect. Yet the Lyceum Speech argues that it is difficult to perpetuate our form of government even in the best of circumstances. Let us see the problem.

Unconventional Piety

Throughout the four or five years prior to Lincoln's Lyceum Speech, resentment had been smoldering in the country. Since the early thirties the agitation of the abolitionists had fanned the coals of resentment against themselves to a white heat, in the North as well as in the South. But when the coals broke into flames of violence, not only the antislavery crusaders were seared. Black or white, abolitionist or slave-owner, outcast or respected citizen, the victims seemed as unpredictable as the violence was contagious. Lincoln's speech records three startling examples. A St. Louis mob seized a free mulatto on suspicion of murder, and actually burned him to death at the stake. A Vicksburg mob hanged three white men, professional gamblers, igniting a blaze of violence which did not end until, as Lincoln says, "dead men were seen literally dangling from the boughs of trees upon every road side." But uppermost in the minds of Lincoln's audience—so that a mere hint in the speech was sufficient to recall it—was the most outrageous act of all. Elijah Lovejoy, the abolitionist editor, was shot dead while trying to defend his printing press from an angry mob. The attention of the nation had been focused on Lovejoy by a series of incidents in which his printing press had three times before been thrown into the Mississippi. In the fourth attack upon him, Lovejoy was killed by a bullet as he tried to defend his press. This shocking murder, which aroused the entire nation, had occurred less than three months before Lincoln spoke. Alton, Illinois, where the murder occurred, was but sixty miles from Springfield. Many in Lincoln's audience sympathized with anti-abolitionist sentiment. Mob violence was not only the subject, but the setting of Lincoln's address.[3]

The Lyceum Speech condemns mob violence and recommends obedience to the laws. This message, however, is but part of an examination of American political institutions. Lincoln points out not only the immediate dangers of mob violence, but also its hidden, long-range dangers to the country's political institutions. He thinks the violence of the 1830's is related to the character of the American regime and believes it threatens that regime. Lincoln's concern is expressed by the title of the speech. It is not, "The Dangers of Mob Violence," but, "The Perpetuation of Our Political Institutions."

(The remedy Lincoln proposes to counter the spreading contagion is that

> . . . reverence for the laws, be breathed by every American mother, to the lisping babe, that prattles on her lap—let it be taught in schools, in seminaries, and in colleges;—let it be written in Primmers (sic), spelling books, and in Almanacs;—let it be preached from the pulpit, proclaimed in legislative halls, and enforced in courts of justice. And, in short, let it become the *political religion* of the nation, and let the old and young, the rich and poor, the grave and the gay, of all sexes and tongues, and colors and conditions, sacrifice unceasingly upon its altars)

Lincoln's call for reverence for the laws is representative of Whig sentiment. What makes it unusual is the argument that precedes it, which shows an uncommon understanding of the political morality of "reverence for the laws." Lincoln shows that an uninstructed passion for justice is an inadequate guide for men's actions. He gives, step by step, a pathology of mob violence, showing that the passions involved in it threaten the political institutions of the country. The danger lies neither in the natural environment nor in political institutions, but in the American propensity toward complacency and illegal violence)

Cosmic and Political Complacency

The members of Lincoln's audience are reluctant to believe that any danger exists to the country's political institutions. The tension of the speech is felt in the wariness with which Lincoln presents the perils he sees, in his repeated return to the question of whether any danger exists, and in his explicit characterization of the views of his audience regarding this threat. He begins by identifying himself and his audience as united in a community of circumstance and opinion:

> In the great journal of things happening under the sun, we, the American People, find our account running, under the date of the nineteenth century of the Christian era. We find ourselves in the peaceful possession, of the fairest portion of the earth, as regards extent of territory, fertility of soil, and salubrity of climate. We find ourselves under the government of a system of political institutions, conducing more essentially to the ends of civil and

religious liberty, than any of which the history of former times tells us. We, when mounting the stage of existence, found ourselves the legal inheritors of these fundamental blessings.

Next he examines the sources of danger. After discounting foreign invasion, Lincoln says "I hope I am over wary; but if I am not, there is, even now, something of ill-omen amongst us." The hesitancy displayed must not make us believe that Lincoln is unsure of his analysis; it reflects that of his audience, not his own. Or, rather, Lincoln identifies himself with the audience through his rhetoric by accepting the audience's hesitancy as his own even at the moment of disagreement.

Not only does Lincoln find it necessary to entice his audience at the beginning, but he has to return continually to this opening theme, for example: "But you are, perhaps ready to ask, 'What has this to do with the perpetuation of our political institutions?' "; or, "I know the American People are *much* attached to their Government;—I know they would suffer *much* for its sake;—I know they would endure evils long and patiently, before they would ever think of exchanging it for another"; or, "But it may be asked, why suppose danger to our political institutions? Have we not preserved them for more than fifty years?" These are only the most obvious of many returns and allusions to the central question of whether any danger exists at all.

We must now return to the passage, quoted above. Lincoln and his audience are all under the same sun, American citizens, contemporaries in the same era, coinhabitants of a fruitful land, under the same government—one more beneficial to civil and religious liberty than any previously known. We note the reiteration of "we find ourselves." All of the unifying factors cited are experienced as gifts which Americans have received and found. They have not created these gifts. These things simply exist and the audience finds itself in possession of them.

The significance of this passive acceptance, and Lincoln's awareness of its significance, can be seen in the introduction of a new element in the last sentence quoted. Lincoln and his audience are the legal inheritors of those blessings. As Lincoln states explicitly, the blessings are theirs because of the actions of their ancestors, actions now preserved in law. The blessings have been secured by men and preserved by men, and, by implication, may be lost by other men.

They are not the unearned and protected gifts of providence or nature. Contrast this political inheritance with the human inheritance described at the beginning. The audience does not recognize the political inheritance as a blessing that requires effort to preserve. Rather, they see it as a gift. They believe they do not possess it only accidentally, but see it as having a place in a greater cosmic scheme. They experience it as happening in the great journal of things under the sun, as part of the Christian era, and as the best part of that era. The audience confuses the political and cosmic condition. They see their political condition as part of the inevitable course of events and fixed scheme of things rather than as the result of human effort calling for continuing efforts at preservation. It requires no effort to gain the things that are already theirs, and so they overlook both the effort originally needed to gain them and the effort needed to sustain them. With cosmic complacency they extend their obliviousness of the work of political creation to passivity in political preservation.

Even if there is no immediate threat, the attitude must be harmful in the long run because it is based upon a false belief that America's land and institutions are not gained and maintained by human effort. Consequently the audience would not be alert to sudden or grave danger.

The Lyceum Speech attempts to overcome complacency by convincing the audience of the actual dangers that exist and of its responsibility for meeting them. The arguments used to convince it of danger must now be examined.

An Aroused Citizenry

Lincoln begins his explicit analysis of the dangers facing the country by citing the increasing incidence of mob violence.[4] He makes clear that it is not merely the outrages of particular mobs that concern him, but the general and growing disposition to disregard the law:

> I hope I am over wary; but if I am not, there is, even now, something of ill-omen amongst us. I mean the increasing disregard for law which pervades the country; the growing disposition to substitute the wild and furious passions, in lieu of the sober judgment of Courts; and the worse than savage mobs, for the executive ministers of justice.

The work of the congress is disregarded, the judgment of the courts gives way to wild and furious passions, and savage mobs take the place of the executive. Behind the threatened replacement of institutions is a change in the disposition of the citizens. By identifying the danger as a new disposition Lincoln places the danger in the men so disposed with two vivid examples.[5]

> In the Mississippi case, they first commenced by hanging the regular gamblers: a set of men, certainly not following for a lifelihood, a very useful, or very honest occupation; but one which, so far from being forbidden by the laws, was actually licensed by an act of the Legislature, passed but a single year before. Next, negroes, suspected of conspiring to raise an insurrection, were caught up and hanged in all parts of the State; then, white men, supposed to be leagued with the negroes; and finally, strangers, from neighboring States, going thither on business, were in many instances, subjected to the same fate. Thus went on this process of hanging, from gamblers to negroes, from negroes to white citizens, and from these to strangers; till, dead men were seen literally dangling from the boughs of trees upon every road side; and in numbers almost sufficient, to rival the native Spanish moss of the country, as a drapery of the forest.

After this florid description of events in Mississippi, Lincoln heightens the horror of the scene by his rapid, sparse outline of the St. Louis story.

> Turn, then to that horror-striking scene at St. Louis. A single victim was only sacrificed there. His story is very short; and is, perhaps, the most highly tragic, of any thing of its length, that has ever been witnessed in real life. A mulatto man, by the name of McIntosh, was seized in the street, dragged to the suburbs of the city, chained to a tree, and actually burned to death; and all within a single hour from the time he had been a freeman, attending to his own business, and at peace with the world.

Such scenes, says Lincoln, have become so common that they no longer attract more attention than an idle remark. But then comes the surprise. Lincoln seems to give in to the prejudices of the audience. The murders were not so bad, after all:

Abstractly considered, the hanging of the gamblers at Vicksburg, was of but little consequence. They constitute a portion of population, that is worse than useless in any community; and their death, if no pernicious example be set by it, is never matter of reasonable regret with anyone. If they were annually swept, from the state of existence, by the plague or small pox, honest man would, perhaps, be much profited, by the operation. Similar too, is the correct reasoning, in regard to the burning of the negro at St. Louis. He had forfeited his life, by the perpetration of an outrageous murder, upon one of the most worthy and respectable citizens of the city; and had he not died as he did, he must have died by the sentence of the law, in a very short time afterwards. As to him alone, it was as well the way it was, as it could otherwise have been.

Not only does Lincoln now say that the lynchings are, abstractly considered, justified, but he also reverses his original characterizations. The law-abiding gamblers are now a worse than useless element of the population. The *mulatto* minding his own business turns out to be a *negro* who has perpetrated an outrageous murder. Lincoln demonstrates, by his speech itself, how easily apathy and complacency may grow. The "mulatto" slides to "negro" and the lawlessness of the burning is excused by the outrageousness of the murder.[6]

Lincoln suggests that the effects of mob law may not always be bad in their immediate results. In fact, a mob may be justifiably incensed over a vile crime, and may know who did the crime, apprehend him, and mete out to him his just punishment. It is possible that such justice in an individual case may be superior to that of the courts, either because there may be some loophole through which the criminal will escape, or, if he does get his just punishment in the end the mob justice is in any event quicker and therefore more just. The use of discretion, even by a mob, may be more exactly just than the general rules of the law.

But Lincoln's position is not that mob action is simply justified, even in those cases where it may be the most immediately just course. On the contrary his argument is that the very justice of a particular example of mob violence may make such violence all the more dangerous. He argues that the example set is a bad one, though the action considered by itself may be good. In the "con-fusion usually attending such transactions, they will be as likely to hang or burn some one, who is neither a gambler nor a murderer as one who is." The innocent are the next to fall, "and thus it goes on, step by step, till all the walls erected for the defense of the persons and property of individuals are trodden down, and disregarded." Mobs should not be entrusted with the enforcement of justice since they are ruled by passion, not cool judgment.

Another danger exists: "the lawless in spirit, are encouraged to become lawless in practice; and having been used to no restraint but dread of punishment, they thus become absolutely unre-strained." And men who love security, seeing their property de-stroyed and families threatened, will become tired and disgusted with a government offering them no protection.

> Thus, then, by the operation of this mobocratic spirit, which all must admit, is now abroad in the land, the strongest bulwark of any Government, and particularly of those constituted like ours, may effectually be broken down and destroyed—I mean the *attachment* of the People.

These dangers of mob law, Lincoln says, are in large part the result of "the proneness of our minds, to regard its direct, as its only consequences." Such proneness is related to the dominance of passion over reason. To examine the long-range consequences of an action requires an escape from passion, for passion is always momentary. While passions may in a particular case be motivated by righteous anger and may result in a particular act of justice, they are nevertheless an unreliable guide because they fail to take into account the long-range consequences. They cannot be depended upon to create justice and must be restrained, if events are not to regress as Lincoln foresees.

Far from restraining passion, righteous indignation may only help to make the passions wild and furious. To seek the immediate implementation of justice may result in even greater injustice, to the point of threatening the destruction of the political institutions of the country. The people must exercise their judgment by giving deference to the law. But this must be done against the "proneness of our minds;" hence it requires an effort. Man's innate rationality backed by passion is insufficient; the mind must be educated to look at indirect consequences.

The Family of the Lion

(If the evil of mob violence springs from a general cause, why did the danger only appear in the 1830's? As Lincoln himself says, "But, it may be asked, why suppose danger to our political institutions? Have we not preserved them for more than fifty years? And why may we not for fifty times as long?" In the second half of the Lyceum Speech, he answers these objections. The evil has not appeared previously because it has been restrained by temporary obstacles. During the early years of the Republic, men's passions had either been channeled into constructive tasks or held in check by the conditions created by the Revolution, but a truly moderate republic had not been established. The Revolution and the peculiar character of the American regime provided a temporary palliative that enabled the country to become established, but did not create the reverence for the laws required for its perpetuation. To show this Lincoln reveals the causes that have restrained the general evil and shows why they no longer can be relied upon. In so doing, he presents the alternatives to political religion which the country had in practice. By showing the inadequacy of these alternatives, he advances our understanding of the need for a political religion. The argument is divided into two parts. First he discusses the ambition of leaders, then the passions of the people.

Leaders who acted from the most intense personal ambition worked coincidentally for the good of their country, to prove a people capable of governing themselves. To a superbly ambitious man, however, presidential or congressional office in an established regime will be an inadequate satisfaction. Many "good men" might be satisfied with such offices,

> . . . but such belong not to the family of the lion, or the tribe of the eagle. What! Think you these places would satisfy an Alexander, a Caesar, or a Napoleon? Never! Towering genius disdains a beaten path. It seeks regions hitherto unexplored. It sees *no distinction* in adding story to story, upon the monuments of fame, erected to the memory of others.

Such men cannot achieve the distinction to which they aspire by merely perpetuating the work of Washington.

(If he cannot gain distinction by aiding the country such a man will do so by harming it. "[Towering genius] thirsts and burns for distinction; and, if possible, it will have it, whether at the expense of emancipating slaves or enslaving freemen." Although he might willingly acquire fame by doing good, ". . . yet, that opportunity being past, and nothing left to be done in the way of building up, he would set boldly to the task of pulling down." This situation did not exist before, when it was yet to be proven that a people were capable of governing themselves.

In portraying this danger, Lincoln draws an implicit distinction between two kinds of ambitious men. The ambition of the first kind is limited by constitutional propriety, and these men are good in that they seek the praise of decent men. They honor the Constitution and seek to earn its rewards. The men of genius are also ambitious, but in a way that separates them qualitatively from men of ordinary ambition. They do not simply seek the praise which men bestow. They know that to accept the praise of men is to subordinate oneself to the standards of other men. They seek distinction, not subordination. Yet they do desire praise. They seek glory without the base alloy of dependence found in ordinary glory by creating the standards by which they are praised and they thereby become the author of the praise bestowed upon themselves.

The danger of moral indifference, which Lincoln finds in the man of genius, also exists in a way in the man of ordinary ambition. Ordinary ambition is morally indifferent not because it transcends the standards of men, but because those standards themselves in the United States reflect moral indifference in their dependence upon novelty and experiment. Lincoln's argument is directed against the danger of a Caesar, and so he exaggerates the uniqueness of Caesar in order to stress the danger from him. Caesar is not so unique that he escapes the standards of men, however. He gains the wonder of men for his actions only because men praise novelty. But wonder is fleeting. A nation seeking novelty will not forever glory in past achievements. The fame of Caesar is at the mercy of future generations, especially when they are not impressed with old successes. Lincoln shows how vulnerable are the reputations of the past. By showing how favorable the circumstances of the founding were, he shows that the achievement of "the Fathers", done to secure fame, is "not much to be wondered at."

The danger of Caesarian ambition, then, is not solely the danger of a great man who is morally indifferent. This danger is partially reflected in the American polity, which favors novelties. As Lincoln was to say in 1859, "Young America . . . has a great passion — a perfect rage — for the 'new'."[9] The ordinary ambitious man of America understands his country as an experiment designed to prove men capable of governing themselves. The American nation is not simply an innocent lamb threatened by the lions of ambition; it is, perhaps, a lamb that sees itself as a lion cub, and hence regards its devourer as a close relative. Lincoln says that men must be tied to the Constituion and laws so as to oppose the threat of a Caesar, but why will men of ordinary ambition adhere to the laws? It is precisely the great man who offers to satisfy their ambition by creating new standards. By attaching themselves to him, they may win the glory they have been taught to seek, this time against the Founders, the very teachers of experimental glory.[10]

The significance of Lincoln's argument lies not only in his portrayal of the ambitious men of genius, but in his picture of the more common love of honor. That love of distinction is open to the manipulation of great men; it is not truly independent. Hence, at base, it is no more moral than the desires of the lions or eagles. One might infer that a political morality whose crowning glory is the man of honor is a defective morality. But this more common man of honor crowns a conventional aristocracy.[11] While Lincoln shows a sense in which men are unequal in the Lyceum speech, his understanding of that inequality is such as to undercut the aristocratic notion that the man of honor is a man of independent virtue.

Earlier, the nation could rest on the support of ambitious men; but now, the very tie which once bound the two together, the conception of the government as experiment, is a threat to the nation. Since the opportunity for achieving novelty by building up has passed, ambitious men of genius will turn to tearing down.

The Passions of the People

The second prop which the country had once, but has no longer, was the effect of the Revolutionary War on the passions of the people. Jealousy, envy, and avarice were for the time being smothered and rendered inactive, ". . . while the deep rooted principles of *hate*, and the powerful motive of *revenge*, instead of being turned against each other, were directed exclusively against the

British nation." Hence the passions of the people were either damp-
ened or directed outside the country.

And thus, from the force of circumstances, the basest principles
of our nature, were either made to lie dormant or to become the
active agents in the advancement of the noblest of causes—that
of establishing and maintaining civil and religious liberty)

While books and speeches will extend the influence of the Revolution, its influence cannot be as great in the future because it
will not be so universally or so vividly felt. Previously every family
had some member who participated in it, perhaps was injured, and
provided a continual reminder of sacrifices made. But Lincoln
knew, as modern statesmen are discovering, that revolutionary
ardor does not last forever)

The love of experimentation could help to found a country
dedicated to liberty, but it could not perpetuate it. The problem, as
Lincoln said at Gettysburg, was not whether such a country could
be created, but whether "this nation, or any nation so conceived
and so dedicated, can long endure.")

The Authority of the Fathers

In the Lyceum Speech Lincoln appeals, as he does throughout his
political life, to the authority of the Founders to support his principles and program, asking every American to swear "by the blood of
the Revolution" (not by the Bible) never to violate the laws. The
people are to pledge their lives, property, and sacred honor to the
Constitution and laws, repeating the pledge of the Founders in the
Declaration of Independence. Furthermore through his own speech
Lincoln tries to strengthen the authority of the Revolution; those
who participated in it:

> . . . were a fortress of strength; but, what invading foemen could
> never do, the silent artillery of time has done the levelling of its
> walls. They are gone. They were a forest of giant oaks, but the
> all-resistless hurricane has swept over them, and left only, here
> and there a lonely trunk, despoiled of its verdure, shorn of its
> foliage unshading and unshaded, to murmur in a few more
> gentle breezes, and to combat with its mutilated limbs, a few
> more ruder storms, then to sink, and be no more.[12]

The men of the Revolution may be no more, but their death is the occasion for recreating their authority. In the penultimate paragraph, Lincoln goes so far as to picture Washington arising at the last judgment to judge the faithfulness with which the people have preserved the freedom he gave them and the reverence with which they have honored him?

Lincoln thus seems to be solving the present difficulties, even while he describes them, by recreating the authority and spirit of that moment in the past when these difficulties did not exist. He points to the unity that existed before the present divisions and thus recalls it. However his appeal to the Fathers is hard to understand. First, how can he do this when he has implied that their authority is suspect and their work imperfect? To return to the past is no solution if the past is partly the cause of the present difficulties. Second, is not his appeal to the Founders merely a temporary expedient? It seems capable of meeting the problem only for the moment, since Lincoln himself has argued that the revolutionary past is fading in memory and that it cannot in future be relied upon to maintian the necessary control of the passions?

Conservatism and Reform

Lincoln clearly does not oppose reform of the law:

> When I so pressingly urge a strict observance of all laws, let me not be understood as saying there are no bad laws, nor that grievances may not arise, for the redress of which, no legal provisions have been made. I mean to say no such thing.

But since he has demonstrated mob law to be worse than the present imperfect law, and that one cannot disobey bad laws without thereby weakening good ones, he advises the following:

> But I do mean to say, that, although bad laws, if they exist, should be repealed as soon as possible, still while they continue in force, for the sake of example, they should be religiously observed. So also in unprovided cases. If such arise, let proper legal provisions be made for them with the least possible delay; but, till then, let them if not too intolerable, be borne with.

There is no inconsistency in Lincoln's appeal to an imperfect past if the most urgent political task is to counteract a present danger

worse than the imperfect past. But an appeal to the past can only be
a temporary barrier against a greater evil. The work of the past itself
must be reformed if a longer range solution is to be found. Lincoln's
solution to this problem is found in the kind of appeal that he
makes to the Founders. He seeks to make the founding a standard
for judging the present. But the Founders serve as a standard not
merely by their achievements—a Constitution and laws—but also
by the example of their actions. Lincoln does not attempt to recreate
the revolutionaries as dead authors or idols but as living judges.
Looking to the past is a way of looking up. Then the appeal to the
past allows for reform of the work of the Founders; indeed, it requires reform. Such reform is not mere destruction, but holds onto
the good while rejecting the evil.

This kind of appeal may be beneficial because in making it,
Lincoln can transmit something of his own, a different understanding of what should be done. Whereas the Founders pledged their
loyalty to the Declaration of Independence, Lincoln calls for loyalty
to the Constitution and laws. He attempts to shift the emphasis
away from the call to independence and novelty which, as we have
seen, was partly the cause of the present troubles. He seeks rather to
instill the obedience and reverence that are necessary to preserve
the benefits the Declaration helped to gain.[12] It is also perhaps not
fanciful to suggest that Lincoln was aware that "fortunes" in the
Founders' pledge may refer not only to estates but to fate, and
purposefully cut out the latter meaning by changing "fortunes" to
"property," shifting the emphasis from novelty and ambition to
preservation and security.

We have seen that Lincoln is so far detached from the Founders
that he questions their lives as well as their work. He was so far from
allowing the revolutionaries to judge him that he took it upon
himself to judge them and their work, and found them wanting.

The appeal to the Revolution thus leaves open the possibility of
reforming the work of the Revolution, provided the country has a
statesman who is detached from the work of the Revolution and is
able to make a creative appeal to it. Such a man must have the
extraordinary judgment of the ambitious man of genius. The statesman Lincoln has described, we might say, would be one of Lincoln's
abilities. In his hands, the true authority derives from his own
wisdom rather than the Founders' doctrines.

The peculiar character of Lincoln's appeal to the past thus partly overcomes the first objection cited. Because fundamental reforms are likely to be for the worse, it is better, by a general presumption for American politics, to preserve the work of the past, although that work is not perfect. Reforms will be for the better in America only when men come on the scene whose understanding and opportunities are superior to those of the Founders. For such men, the authority of the past does not prevent reform. On the contrary, it allows reform because an appeal to the past allows the good to be preserved while exorcising the evil. In ordinary times, political religion preserves the superior spirit of the founding; in the fortunate circumstance of an extraordinary man in power, it becomes an instrument of his reforms. Political religion is a perfect valve, opening and closing as necessary under the direction of a man such as Lincoln.

Revolution and Last Judgment

The second difficulty — that by appealing to the revolutionary spirit, Lincoln invokes an authority whose power is fading — is less adequately dealt with in the Lyceum Speech than in later speeches. However, the direction of Lincoln's solution is suggested here.

The authority of the Revolution is fading, but it can be prolonged through the speech of men like Lincoln, who reawaken awareness of the original sacrifices, thus strengthening and perpetuating their influence. But speech alone is inadequate. Lincoln argues that it was the living veterans of the Revolution, not merely the writings of the Founders, who had had such beneficial results in the early years of the republic. Perhaps a greater oratory than that of the Founders can be a partial substitute for the revolution by offering new examples. Lincoln startlingly attempts to tie the spirit of the Revolution to Biblical religion:

> . . . that we improved to the last; that we remained free to the last; that we revered his name to the last; that, during his long sleep, we permitted no hostile foot to pass over or desecrate his resting place; shall be that which to learn the last trump shall awaken our Washington.

Upon this let the proud fabric of freedom rest, as the rock of its basis; and as truly as has been said of the only greater institution, *'the gates of hell shall not prevail against it.'*)

(He attempts to establish the reverence necessary for preservation by adding the strength of religion—even the fear of hell—to the work of the Founders. This is not the strength of the God of Nature whose laws entitle a people to a separate and equal status among the powers of the earth, but of that religion whose God will hold men to account at the Last Judgment. Lincoln seeks to improve the declining effect of the Revolution by tying the American political institutions to a greater institution that can resist the gates of hell. This suggestion of the Lyceum Speech is not developed in the speech; to understand it we will have to view it in full flower in the Gettysburg Address and the Second Inaugural.)

Reasonable Reverence

(Lincoln has shown the incapacity of reason to govern men by showing the inadequacy of government by wise discretion. His paradoxical example was the case of mob violence, in which the mob might punish more wisely than the law. It is reasonable to rely on law, although law itself is not perfectly reasonable. But law requires support, both because of its unreasonableness in particular instances and because men are not sufficiently reasonable to recognize its long-range reasonableness. This support Lincoln attempts to find in the sacrifices and authority of the Founders. The apparent danger in an appeal to the Founders—the threat of living conservatively or slavishly under the dead letter of the law—is obviated by the excellent work of the Founders and by the character of Lincoln's appeal to them. His appeal allows for reform in circumstances when reform is likely to be beneficial, that is, when a wise man has power. But the authority of the Founders is in need of support. This support can be found in a new political religion that unites Christianity to the work of the Fathers. In the end Americans would have a political religion that ties them to their most reasonable source of common authority, the work of the Founders, while allowing a man of reason, such as Lincoln himself, to improve their work.)

(Furthermore reverence for the laws may be distinguished from either complacency or the passion for justice. While it might seem that to revere the laws is to be complacent, reverence differs from complacency in being open to the element of fear. To be complacent is to lack fear; to reverence is possibly to fear attack upon the revered. Hence complacency does not search into things, but reverence may both look for danger and search for new reasons to revere. The man who has reverence for the laws will be more open to the long-range threats to the law that Lincoln presents in the Lyceum Speech than will one who is complacent.

The passion for justice, on the other hand, seeks immediate gratification and lacks a clear standard; reverence for the laws finds a standard in the laws and reins in the passion for immediate gratification by honoring the procedures of the law.

Hence reason (Lincoln) can furnish all the materials (the uniting of the Biblical tradition to the work of the Founders) for the country's future defense and support. Lincoln looks to the rule of reason, but he also looks to the passionate means whereby the passions may be so moderated that reason may be effective. Men's habits must be formed in a way that allows scope for reason. The materials furnished by reason must produce "general intelligence, sound morality, and reverence for the Constitution and laws," and not merely or especially intellectual brilliance.

We have seen Lincoln's analysis of the problem facing the country in the 1830's. This problem was not merely a temporary aberration, but reflected certain defects in the very foundations of the country. The Lyceum Speech does not fully reveal—or at least, does not fully explicate—Lincoln's proposed solution to the problems he saw. However, the Lyceum Speech does reveal the main elements of Lincoln's later solution, and their apparent lack of harmony within the Lyceum Speech provides us with a clue to the problems Lincoln's solution entailed.

III.
EQUALITY AND JUSTICE

(In the preceeding chapter we have seen that Lincoln's Lyceum Speech argues that the mob violence of the 1830's stemmed from causes found in the fundamental political order of the country, in its inadequate attraction for men of ambition and its failure to find a substitute for the spirit of the revolution. A man of genius could well seize the occasion to subvert the country's political institutions. What, then, is the character of Lincoln's support of democracy and how is it related to his political religion? Citizens and scholars have agreed that Lincoln is the greatest statesman associated with the cause of popular government.[1] While Americans in particular have revered his name, they are not alone in admiring him. Of the great statesmen of modern democracy Lincoln alone seems inseparable from democracy. One can easily imagine Churchill, for example, also leading his country in more aristocratic times. But it is difficult to see Lincoln in such a setting. Yet the nature of his association with the cause of democracy remains obscure.)

(Common opinion has regarded Lincoln as the perfect democractic man. Lincoln was a man of the people and he had faith in the people. He was a man of the people not only because he was born in a log cabin, but because he had the same virtues as the people, although to an uncommon degree. Honest Abe was so virtuous that he would walk miles to return pennies. This was extraordinary, but not inexplicable. Honesty is a virtue everyone understands—everyone knows that one should return an overcharge. It is only extraordinary that Lincoln should be so virtuous in such a small matter at such great expense to himself. One needs an uncommon degree of the common virtues to be a great man or a great President, but Lincoln shows that one does not need virtues of a different—perhaps more aristocratic—order. Greatness is rare but not beyond the reach of democratic man.)

(Lincoln had faith in the people. The author of a recent biography of Lincoln confirms the popular opinion when he writes, "The people's composite wisdom and moral rectitude had proved to be surer guides [than the judgments of supposedly great minds], and he had deferred to mass opinion, firm in the conviction that the people were trustworthy, when informed."[2] Democracy is not simply expedient—Lincoln did not support it simply because it existed and could not be changed without great upheavals, if at all. Nor is democracy based upon an assertion of unappealable authority— that the people have the right to authorize the laws because it is their consent that establishes the just powers of government. Rather democracy is good because the people in the aggregate are wiser and more moral than any alternative ruling body of the few or one. They choose more wisely and can be expected to make sounder decisions when properly informed.)

Democracy regards Lincoln not merely as its champion, but as its vindicator. Popular opinion in America has not simply praised Lincoln, it has venerated him. This veneration is inexplicable except on the supposition that popular opinion dimly believes that something surpassing itself has vindicated itself. One does not venerate beings of the same order as oneself. Men look up, and in looking up, catch a ray of light from a star they cannot know. They may regard the source as but another example of earthly fire moving according to well-known or discoverable laws. Yet even so, that dim light pales mere earth-bound flames and its movement compels at least the faithful to ask, "What is man, that Thou art mindful of him?" Veneration of Lincoln is inexplicable on the common assumption that he did not transcend the common virtues and hence that he did not transcend democracy in some way. The popular opinion of Lincoln has lain between pride and wonder.

Few, if any, students of Lincoln have been as aware as Woodrow Wilson of Lincoln's distrust of common judgment, and of the wisdom and moral rectitude of the people as sure guides. In one of his speeches on Lincoln, Wilson almost contemptuously reminds his listeners and us, "A great nation is not led by a man who simply repeats the talk of the street-corners or the opinions of the newspapers."[3] Nevertheless Wilson believed that Lincoln was properly regarded as a man of the people, one "who has his rootage deep in the experiences and consciousness of the ordinary mass of his fellow-men," and

. . . drawing his sap from such sources, has, nevertheless, risen above the level of the rest of mankind and has got an outlook over their heads, seeing horizons which they are too submerged to see; a man who finds and draws his inspiration from the common plane, but nevertheless has lifted himself to a new place of outlook and of insight; who has come out from the people and is their leader, not because he speaks from their ranks, but because he speaks for them and for their interests.[4]

The man of the people does not merely see what the people see, but stands above them by virtue of his superior outlook and insight. Yet he has not simply separated himself from the rest. Rather he draws his sap from the experiences and consciousness of the ordinary mass; he finds his inspiration from the common plane.

Wilson interprets the broader horizons of a man of the people in a particular way. He explains:

A great nation is not led by a man who simply repeats the talk of the street-corners or the opinions of the newspapers. A nation is led by a man who hears more than those things; or who, rather, hearing those things, understands them better, unites them, puts them into· a common meaning; speaks, not the rumors of the street, but a new principle for a new age; a man in whose ears the voices of the nation do not sound like the accidental and discordant notes that come from the voice of a mob, but concurrent and concordant like the united voices of a chorus, whose many meanings, spoken by melodious tongues, unite in his understanding in a single meaning and reveal to him a single vision, so that he can speak what no man else knows, the common meaning of the common voice.[5]

The man of the people does not simply see things which the people do not see or see the same things more clearly, but he expresses the common meaning behind the discord of common speech. The act of the man of the people is not fundamentally an act of sight which would separate him from his fellow men, but an expressive act. He does not see the world more clearly but reveals the previously unseeable world. This world is already present in the discordant voices of the people; it only needs to be understood and articulated. There is a unity beneath the discord of speech which can be found and articulated, turning the discord of many into the harmony of a chorus. The man of the people shares with the people this pre-verbal unity and articulates it for them. In the man of the people the unconscious nation becomes conscious.)

If one asks what assurance there is that this preverbal unity exists and that the unity created by Lincoln's speech is not imposed by him, Wilson would answer that this unity is not conventional, but potentially always exists. This unity is not simply that of a nation, which may or may not exist, but that of humanity itself:

> And then, last and greatest characteristic of all, a man of the people is a man who has felt that unspoken, that intense, that almost terrifying struggle of humanity, that struggle whose object is, not to get forms of government, not to realize particular formulas or make for any definite goal, but simply to live and to be free. . . . He has, therefore, felt beat in him, if he had any heart, a universal sympathy for those who struggle, a universal understanding of the unutterable things that were in their hearts and the unbearable burdens that were upon their backs.[6]

A man of the people is one who has shared the unspeakable struggle for life. Not forms of government, but the struggle of humanity is the crucial focus. The common source of the common man and Lincoln is life itself, nobly interpreted. Lincoln is the universal and therefore preeminent man and democracy is the universal and therefore preeminent state. Lincoln is not a partisan nor is democracy merely a particular form of government. Rather both represent life itself, not a particular end for life.)

Wilson seeks a democratic interpretation of Lincoln. He tries to grant Lincoln's superior wisdom without thereby undermining Lincoln's association with the common man. He does not find Lincoln's unity with the people in the fact that Lincoln shares the virtues of the common man, such as honesty. He rather finds the common struggle for life to be represented both by democracy and by Lincoln. Democracy is not conventional, and the unity of all men cannot be broken by forms of government.)

This understanding is not that of Lincoln himself. Rather, as we shall attempt to show, Lincoln considered democracy to be conventional in an important sense. It is true that he did not regard specific institutions to be the essence of democracy, but he did regard a particular opinion to be so. Lincoln's support of democracy is closer to common understanding as we have outlined it than it is to that of Wilson)

The Almost Chosen People

(As common opinion implicitly recognizes in venerating Lincoln, his support of democracy is complex and problematic. Yet Lincoln's support of democracy, we repeat, is akin to that of the people. He not only asks the same question concerning democracy that the people ask, but he agrees with them on the criteria by which the answer shall be judged. To the question, Is democracy good?, common opinion answers, Yes, because the people are wise and just. Lincoln, too, in the moment when American democracy was put to its greatest test, thought democracy to be finally good only if the people are wise and just. Lincoln did not shrink from saying in his First Inaugural, given on the eve of civil war:

> Why should there not be a patient confidence in the ultimate justice of the people? . . . If the Almighty ruler of nations, with his eternal truth and justice, be on your side of the North or on yours of the South, that truth, and that justice, will surely prevail, by the judgment of this great tribunal, the American people.)

(If the people are not ultimately just, then there is no reason other than expediency why they should decide questions of justice. There was no reason why the South should stay in the Union unless that Union were just. If the people were not just, neither was the Union founded on the assertion that governments derive their just powers from the consent of the governed. Lincoln did not shrink from facing the question whether the majority were just, nor from the answer that they were. The voice of the American people is ultimately equivalent to the voice of God, because the American people is a just tribunal)

(We need not be naive. In the Second Inaugural Lincoln asserts that the judgments of God are not those of men. Harry Jaffa raises the question, "Did this not mean that Lincoln had been wrong in supposing, as he did in the earlier utterance, that the voice of the people was the voice of God?"[8] Jaffa's answer to his rhetorical question is implicitly, yes. Yet the words of the First Inaugural are insufficient to answer this question definitively. Lincoln does not assert that the voice of the people is always the voice of God. He asserts that the voice of God will ultimately prevail as the voice of the American people on the particular issue dividing North from South. The grounds for this assertion are not clear. To raise just one cynical possibility, is it surprising that Lincoln asserts the people will decide justly when it is Lincoln who is in a position to lead and guide them? Would he have said the same thing had he lost the election? Certainly Lincoln is appealing to the democratic tendency to regard the voice of the people as the voice of God, but whether he fully shares that opinion is unclear because he was well aware that the people might decide wrongly. When the possibility that he might be outvoted was once presented to him, Lincoln replied:

> The *probability* that we may fall in the struggle *ought not* to deter us from the support of a cause we believe to be just; it *shall not* deter me. If ever I feel the soul within me elevate and expand to those dimensions not wholly unworthy of its Almighty Architect, it is when I contemplate the cause of my country, deserted by all the world beside, and I standing up boldly and alone and hurling defiance at her victorious oppressors.[9]

Not only does Lincoln separate the cause of his country from the opinion or support of the people, he even indicates that he would come closest to God in such a situation.

Lincoln's actions prior to the War are equally revealing, for they belie the confidence in the justice of the people that he apparently expresses in the First Inaugural. His fight with Douglas, above all, can only be explained on the assumption that there was a real possibility that the American people could be wrong. Lincoln pictured his struggle against Douglas as an attempt to prevent an evil opinion—that slavery was either a positive good or at least not an evil—from being accepted by the people. If there was no possibility of its acceptance, then there was no point in fighting Douglas. But further, he would then be culpable for creating a bitter quarrel leading to civil war over a matter of no practical importance. Lincoln's opinions and actions before he became President assert and imply that the people can be wrong.[10]

Nor is it the case that Lincoln thought the people merely needed to be informed in order to judge rightly. After calling for reliance upon the great tribunal of the American people in the First Inaugural, Lincoln goes on to say, "While the people retain their virtue, and vigilance, no administration, by any extreme of wickedness or folly, can very seriously injure the government, in the short space of four years." Yet these words themselves indicate Lincoln saw the possibility of the people losing their virtue and vigilance. This is a problem that occupied him from the time of his earliest speeches. The Lyceum Speech, as we have seen, examines the loss of vigilance among the people since the time of the Revolution, and questions whether they are, or have been, virtuous.

The tension in Lincoln's thought between his support of popular government and his awareness that the people might not be just was accurately expressed on his way to Washington in 1861, when he referred to the American people as the Almighty's "almost chosen people."[11] Democracy presupposes the people's justice, yet the justice of the American people is not certain. Lincoln not only expresses the tension, but points toward his resolution of the difficulty in this phrase. God has favored these people—perhaps they may yet become his chosen people. Only if God chooses the American people, is the American democracy unqualifiedly just. We must examine more carefully Lincoln's support for democracy.

Democracy and Slavery

In a fragment whose context or occasion we do not know, Lincoln once defined democracy. Although it now appears accidental, the purity of the definition does not allow us to suppose that it was but an off-hand scribble. It bears the mark of the peculiar deliberation and precision characteristic of Lincoln's most mature and greatest writings. It reveals that Lincoln considered the question of slavery to be intimately related to the problem of democracy. Wrote Lincoln: "As I would not be a slave, so I would not be a master. This expresses my idea of democracy. Whatever differs from this, to the extent of the difference, is no democracy."[12]

If we are to believe Socrates' description of the democratic city in Plato's *Republic* and Glaucon's implication that it paralleled Athenian practice, we may suspect that there was a tension between ancient democracy and slavery.[13] It nevertheless remains true that ancient democracy was compatible with slavery because it was based on the equality of freeborn men, not on the equality of all men.[14] There is no doubt, then, that Lincoln's definition refers to modern democracy, but it is less clear whether the definition em bodies a modern *understanding* of modern democracy.)

(According to the definition, democracy consists of a choice and a reason for that choice. The choice a modern democrat makes is not to be a master. Ancient democrats refused to be slaves, but were glad to be masters and even saw their dignity there)

The modern democrat, according to Lincoln, refuses to be a master for a particular reason—because he would not be a slave. Lincoln gives the major premise and conclusion of the democrat's syllogism, but we shall have to supply the minor premise. The major premise is, I would not be a slave. The conclusion is, therefore I would not be a master. Clearly, the minor premise must establish equivalence between being a master and being a slave. Why, from the position of democracy, is being a master equivalent to being a slave? Why does recognition of this equality in one's choices make one a democrat?)

To answer these questions, we must examine Lincoln's opinions concerning slavery)

Negro Slavery

In a letter written in October, 1858, Lincoln enclosed clippings that, he said, contained the substance of all he had ever said about "negro equality."[15] The clippings comprise extracts from five of Lincoln's speeches. He did not say they contained all he had ever thought about "negro equality." Yet Lincoln continually repeated the substance, and even the exact words of these extracts; they represent his considered and mature public judgment on the question. The earliest of the clippings is from a speech given in reply to one by Douglas in Peoria on October 16, 1854. In it, Lincoln states three reasons for his opposition to the spread of slavery:

> This *declared* indifference [of Douglas], but as I must think, covert *real* zeal for the spread of slavery, I can not but hate. I hate it because it deprives our republican example of its just influence in the world—enables the enemies of free institutions, with plausibility, to taunt us as hypocrites—causes the real friends of freedom to doubt our sincerity, and especially because it forces so many really good men amongst ourselves into an open war with the very fundamental principles of civil liberty—criticizing the Declaration of Indepedence, and insisting that there is no right principle of action but *self-interest.*[16])

These three reasons — that slavery itself is monstrously unjust, that it subverts our republican example, and that it forces good men into open war with the principles of civil liberty — are repeated with variations in the other clippings. The second reason is primarily — though not wholly — expediential. It is the third reason, and its relationship to the first, that really concerns us. Lincoln says he hates slavery especially for the reason that it causes good men to turn away from the Declaration of Independence and to hold the opinion that there is no right principle of action but self-interest. The alternative to believing slavery unjust is to believe that there is no justice at all, and that the only right principle of action is self-interest. We must try to understand why Lincoln thought that all morality is destroyed when slavery is considered just.

Lincoln's opposition to slavery was always on fundamentally moral grounds, though he was willing to use reasons of expediency. It was to the moral question that he continually reverted. He saw Douglas's vaunted indifference to the slavery question as refusal to face the moral problem. Douglas could do this only by explicitly or implicitly denying that the negro was human. In a speech delivered in Memphis, Tennessee, in 1858, and on several other occasions, Douglas had declared that "in all contests between the negro and the white man, he was for the white man, but that in all questions between the negro and the crocodile he was for the negro." Lincoln interpreted this to be:

> . . . a sort of proposition in proportion, which may be stated thus: As the negro is to the white man, so is the crocodile to the negro, and as the negro may rightfully treat the crocodile as a beast or reptile, so the white man may rightfully treat the negro as a beast or reptile.[17]

Yet, Lincoln argued, not only was the negro a man, but Judge Douglas, despite his insinuations, knew that he was a man. So did the South. If the negro were not a man, why had the South joined the North almost unanimously in abolishing the slave trade and annexing to it the punishment of death; why had it despised the slave-dealer; and how could slaves be freed?[18] Once admit the negro is a man, then the relationship of man to his sub-human property is irrelevant.

(If the negro is a man, there is no principle upon which negro slavery may be justified unless white men are enslaved as well:

> If A can prove, however conclusively, that he may, of right, enslave B.—why may not B. snatch the same argument, and prove equally, that he may enslave A? —
>
> You say A. is white, and B. is black. It is *color,* then; the lighter, having the right to enslave the darker? Take care. By this rule, you are to be a slave to the first man you meet, with a fairer skin than your own.
>
> You do not mean *color* exactly?—You mean the whites are *intellectually* the superiors of the blacks, and, therefore have the right to enslave them? Take care again. By this rule, you are to be slave to the first man you meet, with an intellect superior to your own.
>
> But, say you, it is a question of *interest;* and if you can make it your *interest,* you have the right to enslave another. Very well. And if he can make it his interest, he has the right to enslave you.[19]

One cannot corrupt the moral relationship between white men and black men without also corrupting relations among white men because there is no moral principle separating one group from the other. One knows the negro to be a man. To treat him as a beast prepares one to treat other men as beasts)

Slavery

One may argue that the practical alternative facing the country was adherence to the Declaration or surrender to self-interest, because belief in negro slavery was tantamount to the second possibility. But Lincoln's opposition did not extend merely to negro slavery. He opposed all slavery. The alternative to this opposition, he said, was not some other moral principle, but no moral principle at all. The connection between opposition to slavery *per se* and a just political order is more fundamental than that between the latter and negro slavery. Yet this connection is not simply that slavery is unjust. Said Lincoln:

> In his [Douglas's] view, the question of whether a new country shall be slave or free, is a matter of as utter indifference, as it is

whether his neighbor shall plant his farm with tobacco, or stock it with horned cattle. Now, whether this view is right or wrong, it is very certain that the great mass of mankind take a totally different view. They consider slavery a great moral wrong; and their feelings against it, are not evanescent, but eternal. It lies at the very foundation of their sense of justice; and it cannot be trifled with. It is a great and durable element of popular action, and I think, no statesman can safely disregard it.[20]

It is important to determine what Lincoln means when he says that opposition to slavery lies at the foundation of the popular sense of justice. In saying that no statesman can disregard opposition to slavery, he surely means that it is a powerful feeling. On other occasions, Lincoln pointed out that the actions of government are limited by the vehement opinions and prejudices of the people. For example, in examining whether the negro should be made the political and social equal of the white, Lincoln notes that the feelings of the great mass of white people would rebel against it. He goes on to say: "Whether this feeling accords with justice and sound judgment, is not the sole question, if indeed, it is any part of it. A universal feeling, whether well or ill-founded, can not be safely disregarded. We can not, then, make them equals.[21] But opposition to slavery is sufficiently powerful that no statesman can disregard it, regardless of its justice or injustice.

Richard Hofstadter notes the similarity between the two preceding quotations, and suggests that Lincoln's political opposition to slavery was due to the calculation of political forces which the quotations reveal him to be making.[22] While Hofstadter improves our understanding of Lincoln's political shrewdness, it is even more important to note the differences between the statements. From the first statement one cannot conclude anything about the cause of Lincoln's opposition to slavery, because the argument would equally lead one to support slavery. It touches only the point of whether a statesman can be indifferent to slavery, not whether he should support or oppose it. One cannot be indifferent. More important, however, the two statements do suggest a difference between popular feelings against slavery and against making the negro the social and political equal of the white. The former is not merely a universal feeling, as is the latter, but the very foundation of the sense of justice in the great mass of mankind.

Opposition to slavery lies at the foundation of the popular sense of justice, which Lincoln does not doubt is a true perception of justice.

To see why Lincoln considers opposition to slavery the foundation of justice in this sense, we must first note the obvious, that slavery is contrary to the principle that all men are created equal. In a speech delivered in June, 1857, in Springfield, Lincoln gave his interpretation of the phrase, "all men are created equal." In the first place, contrary to Douglas's assertion, the authors of the Declaration of Independence meant to include all men; and, second, they specified in what respects they considered all men to be created equal:

> They did not mean to say all were equal in color, size, intellect, moral developments, or social capacity. They defined with tolerable distinctness, in what respects they did consider all men created equal—equal in "certain unalienable rights, among which are life, liberty, and the pursuit of happiness."[23]

This did not mean that the Founders thereupon secured these rights for all men. "They meant simply to declare the right, so that the enforcement of it might follow as fast as circumstances should permit." They did this not for the sake of effecting a separation from Great Britain, for which "it was of no practical use," but:

> They meant to set up a standard maxim for free society, which should be familiar to all, and revered by all; constantly looked to, constantly labored for, and even though never perfectly attained, constantly approximated, and thereby constantly spreading and deepening its influence, and augmenting the happiness and value of life to all people of all colors everywhere.[24]

In the light of the Declaration, then, the question was not whether the negro was equal in color, moral development, or intellectual endowments to the white man. The question was merely whether the negro was a man. If he was a man, he was entitled to the rights which apply to man as man. Hence Lincoln concluded:

> . . . there is no reason in the world why the negro is not entitled to all the natural rights enumerated in the Declaration of Independence, the right to life, liberty, and the pursuit of happiness. I hold that he is as much entitled to these as the white man. I

agree with Judge Douglas he is not my equal in many respects
—certainly not in color, perhaps not in moral or intellectual en-
dowment. But in the right to eat the bread, without leave of
anybody else, which his own hand earns, *he is my equal and the
equal of Judge Douglas and the equal of every living man.*[25]

The principle that all men are created equal is the father of all
morality in the people, as Lincoln repeated on many occasions.[26]
Hence we may narrow our inquiry to the reason why this is the
foundation of popular morality.

Equality and Public Opinion

If one can change the public belief in equality, one has made the
crucial change towards destroying popular morality. Lincoln puts it
this way:

> Our government rests in public opinion. Whoever can change
> public opinion, can change the government, practically just as
> much. Public opinion, on any subject, always has a "central idea,"
> from which all its minor thoughts radiate. That "central idea" in
> our political public opinion, at the beginning was, and until re-
> cently has continued to be, "the equality of men." And although
> it was always submitted patiently to whatever of inequality there
> seemed to be as matter of actual necessity, its constant working
> has been a steady progress towards the practical equality of
> all men.[27]

Public opinion is crucial in a democracy because it is the dominant
opinion. Whether right or wrong, it will tend to spread and will
constantly affect practical actions. This does not mean that public
opinion is necessarily untrue; it does mean that even truth needs
support from dominant opinion to be effective.

Now the American union represents a public commitment to
justice. It is founded on the popular sense of justice, whose central
idea is the equality of all men. In a speech delivered in Chicago on
July 10, 1858, Lincoln attempted to explain the tie between union
and equality. In explaining why we celebrate the Fourth of July,
he says that we try to explain our present prosperity by looking
back to:

. . . a race of men living in that day whom we claim as our fathers and grandfathers; they were iron men, they fought for the principle that they were contending for; and we understand that by what they then did it has followed that the degree of prosperity that we now enjoy has come to us. We hold this annual celebration to remind ourselves of all the good done in this process of time, of how it was done and who did it, and how we are historically connected with it; and we go from these meetings in better humor with ourselves — we feel more attached the one to the other, and more firmly bound to the country we inhabit.[28]

But to look back to "a race of men living in that day whom we claim as our fathers and grandfathers" would not necessarily unite us the one to the other. "We have not yet reached the whole." After all, we have many citizens who cannot look back to those men as their fathers and grandfathers. They, or their ancestors, have come from Europe since the Revolution. They have no common ties of blood to that earlier race which would connect them to us.

. . . but when they look through that old Declaration of Independence they find that those old men say that "We hold these truths to be self-evident, that all men are created equal," and then they feel that that moral sentiment taught in that day evidences their relation to those men, that it is the father of all moral principle in them, and that they have a right to claim it as though they were blood of the blood, and flesh of the flesh of the men who wrote the Declaration, and so they are. That is the electric cord in that Declaration that links the hearts of patriotic and liberty-loving men together, that will link those patriotic hearts as long as the love of freedom exists in the minds of men throughout the world.[29]

The Union can assimilate newcomers because it is based on a principle that is the father of morality in men. This principle has not been forced upon the American people, for it is rooted in the way men are. We do not have a union because of a common history, but we have a common history because the Union is the triumph of moral principle within ourselves. Furthermore, the Union is not only *a* moral union, but founded as it is on the basic principle of popular morality, it is *the* moral union.

The relationship between the Union and equality, therefore, is complex. First, the Union is good because it is founded on the basic principle of popular morality. Lincoln always made it clear that in working for the preservation of the Union, he was not so much working for the mere adherence of one state to another as he was working for the principle upon which the Union was based. He always maintained that the "Union must be preserved in the purity of its principles as well as in the integrity of its territorial parts."[30] If the territorial union could be saved only by giving up the principles of the Declaration, Lincoln once said, "I would rather be assassinated on this spot than to surrender it."[31]

While the principle that all men are created equal thus may be said to be prior to the Union, in a second sense, the Union is prior to the principle. The principle, as we have seen, requires public support to be effective. The Union, then, is not merely a possible means to the principle's actualization; it is the necessary means. Now if a means is necessary, it takes on something of the quality of an end, since it is no longer a matter of prudence whether this particular means is chosen. Thus the principle that all men are created equal requires the Union to make it effective. There seems to be a circle: the government depends upon public opinion, but public opinion depends upon the government. In the Lyceum Speech, Lincoln attributes the original solution of this chicken and egg problem not to the people, but to a few men who proved that a people could govern themselves.[32]

There were some, the Abolitionists, who would have destroyed the Union for the sake of maintaining the principle of equality in its purity. They did not merely neglect the fact that Lincoln was willing to preserve the Union only on the ground of equality; more importantly, they neglected the fact that the Union was the necessary means to the end of equality. That the preservation of the Union was necessary to the advancement of equality in practice should have been evident. Defenders of the nobility of the abolitionist passion must face the hard fact that equality would not have been advanced by the South's becoming a separate country. The prospects of equality for the negro, however dim, were infinitely greater if the South remained a part of the Union dedicated to the principle that all men are created equal. Lincoln shows that this practical connection was based on a theoretical connection. The principle of equality needs public support because human reason is insufficient to make men just.

Equality and Justice

Justice depends on public opinion in a democracy. The question then is: What is the highest degree of justice public opinion will support? Is this degree the same as the highest degree of justice *per se*?

Lincoln's answer to the first question is justice based on the equality of all men. Let us suppose, as he suggests in the Lyceum Speech, that there is a race of men who belong to the "family of the lion, or the tribe of the eagle." [32] The virtues of these men are qualitatively different from the virtues of the rest of mankind. In such a case it is not just to give these men what would be given to others, because equal portions are not justly distributed to unequal persons. Justice demands that their natural superiority be recognized.

But the Lyceum Speech reveals that the people cannot recognize this superiority. How can they distinguish transcendent virtues from transcendent vices? Napoleon may appear as much their champion as Lincoln.

Lincoln once explained the difficulty of deciding who is a slave as follows:

> . . . we will suppose the Rev. Dr. Ross has a slave named Sambo, and the question is "Is it the Will of God that Sambo shall remain a slave, or be set free?" The Almighty gives no audible answer to the question, and his revelation—the Bible—gives none—or, at most, none but such as admits of a squabble, as to its meaning. No one thinks of asking Sambo's opinion on it. So, at last, it comes to this, that Dr. Ross is to decide the question. And while he considers it, he sits in the shade, with gloves on his hands, and subsists on the bread that Sambo is earning in the burning sun. If he decides that God Wills Sambo to continue a slave, he thereby retains his own comfortable position; but if he decides that God wills Sambo to be free, he thereby has to walk out of the shade, throw off his gloves, and delve for his own bread. Will Dr. Ross be actuated by that perfect impartiality, which has ever been considered most favorable to correct decisions? [33]

We can now return to Lincoln's definition of democracy, "As I would not be a slave, so I would not be a master." The reason why slavery equals mastership is now clear. In a democracy, the true grounds of inequality are invisible. Democracy is founded on public opinion, which must reinforce the popular sense of justice. Public opinion cannot distinguish real inequality from the great pretenders of inequality; however, it can recognize equality. Then the only security against becoming a slave to others is to deny oneself mastership over others. To claim to be a master asserts an inequality which public opinion cannot accurately assay, and hence prepares the ground for one's own enslavement.

For the same reason, the definition suggests that the relationship between master and slave is equivalent to the relationship between ruler and ruled: the

> . . . argument of the Judge is the same old serpent that says you work and I eat, you toil and I will enjoy the fruits of it. Turn it whatever way you will—whether it comes from the mouth of a King, an excuse for enslaving the people of his country, or from the mouth of men of one race as a reason for enslaving the men of another race, it is all the same old serpent.[34]

We can now understand why Lincoln believes that holding slavery to be good is destructive of all morality in a democracy. One cannot hold the opinion without destroying the belief in equality, but to destroy the belief in equality is to destroy the only foundation of popular justice in a democracy.

Equality and Democracy

In the Lyceum Speech Lincoln raised the possibility of the relevant inequality among men. Did he in fact believe that there are men who belong to "the tribe of the eagle?" Harry Jaffa has presented a convincing argument, based largely on the Lyceum Speech, that Lincoln knew them to exist.[35] Briefly it is this. In tacitly denying the greatness of the Founders' work and motives in the Lyceum Speech, Lincoln shows that the thirst for enduring fame which he attributes to the "family of the lion" is itself destructive. It can be undermined by succeeding generations as Lincoln undermines the fame of the Founders. Lincoln thus shows disdain not only for the ordinary praise of men, but even for that love of fame which is the "ruling passion of the noblest minds." He thereby reveals that he does not consider political good to be the highest good and thus transcends the sphere of politics.

However this may be, Lincoln's views are characterized by rejection of every form of government other than democracy. In the same speech in which he says that opposition to slavery is at the foundation of the popular sense of justice, he says that at the foundation of his own sense of justice lay his "faith in the proposition that each man should do precisely as he pleases with all which is exclusively his own."[36] This proposition Lincoln identifies as the principle of self-government.

In defining self-government, Lincoln clearly thinks of its political, rather than its strictly moral, sense. If everyone may do what he will with whatever is exclusively his own, then he is self-governing in the political sense. Now this may be seen as implied in the principle of the Declaration of Independence that all men are created equal — that all men have certain unalienable rights which they may utilize in any way they want. However, Lincoln also says, "Give ALL the governed an equal voice in the government, and that, and that only is self-government."[37] Now these two principles of self-government are not identical — the one that all men equally have unalienable rights, and the other that all men have an equal voice in the government. The Gettysburg Address associates them. At the end of the speech the nation conceived in liberty and dedicated to the proposition that all men are created equal, has become "government of the people, by the people, for the people." But the Declaration is indifferent to forms of government except, possibly, in excluding absolute monarchy and tyranny; rather, it explicitly says that the People, in instituting a new government, have the right of "laying its foundations on such principles and organizing its powers in such form, as to them shall seem most likely to effect their Safety and Happiness." Further, in listing the tyrannical actions of George III, it implies that his would be a legitimate government if he had not overstepped the bounds of limited monarchy. The fact that he was a king is not one of the objections made to him. That all men are created equal does not necessarily lead to government "of the people, by the people, for the people."[38] Now Lincoln, while admitting the possibility of the rare man who rises above the mass, rejects the more usual kinds of aristocratic virtue. Lincoln's thorough-going democratic sympathies are evident from his speech delivered before the Washington Temperance Society of Springfield in 1842. Members of this society were a then new kind of reformers, that is, former drunkards.

The Proper Champions of Temperance

⟨In the temperance speech Lincoln asks why the temperance movement is successful in 1842 when it had failed in the past. In answer he argues that both the champions of temperance and the tactics they use are better than in the past. Because the old reformers are composed chiefly of preachers, lawyers, and hired agents, they suffer from a want of approachability to the mass of mankind. Now these men might be said to be the democratic "aristocrats." They are the *Federalist's* "men of learned professions," who are able to win the confidence of the entire community.[39] But the preacher appears to be a fanatic who desires the union of church and state; the lawyer a vain man who wishes to hear himself speak; and the hired agent a man out for his pay. None of them seemingly has at heart the interest of those whom they would reform.⟩

⟨In contrast, it is difficult, if not impossible, to ascribe ulterior motives to the new champions:

> But when one, who has long been known as a victim of intemperance bursts the fetters that have bound him and appears before his neighbors "clothed, and in his right mind," a redeemed specimen of long lost humanity, and stands up with tears of joy trembling in his eyes, to tell of the miseries *once* endured, *now* to be endured no more forever; of his once naked and starving children, now clad and fed comfortably; of a wife long weighed down with woe, weeping, and a broken heart, now restored to health, happiness, and renewed affections; and how easily it all is done, once it is resolved to be done; however simple his language, there is a logic, and an eloquence to it, that few, with human feelings, can resist.[40]

The democratic reformer must both sympathize with those to be reformed and be an object of sympathy in return.⟩

The Proper Tactics of Reform

⟨The first fault in the tactics of the old reformers, Lincoln notes, was that they indulged in impolitic and unjust denunciation: "it is not much in the nature of man to be driven to any thing; still less to be driven about that which is exclusively his own business; and least of all, where such driving is to be submitted to, at the expense of pecuniary interest or buring appetite." The old reformers spoke as does a lordly judge to a felon just before he passes punishment of death. It "is not wonderful that they were slow, *very slow* to acknowledge the truth of such denunciations." To have expected otherwise was to expect a reversal of human nature "which is God's decree, and can never be reversed."[41]

Persuasion, not denunciation, is the means which must be used. Convince a person that you are his sincere friend and then it is possible to reason with him, providing your cause is just. Without friendship, even truth will fail. "If you would win a man to your cause, *first* convince him that you are his sincere friend. Therein is a drop of honey that catches his heart, which, say what he will, is the great high road to his reason."[42] Lincoln says further, "In my judgment, such of us as have never fallen victims, have been spared more from the absence of appetite, than from any mental or moral superiority over those who have."[43] By itself a stronger appetite neither associates nor disassociates a man from the moral community. Indeed the same peculiarity that makes such persons liable to the degradation of drunkenness gives them the possibility of being the mental and moral superiors of their fellows. The strength of the appetites by itself is simply a naturally given factor which differs from individual to individual without in itself affecting moral worth. Lincoln therefore rejects the aristocratic moral claims of the old temperance movement.

The Injustice of Denunciation

Lincoln leads to his second argument—that it is unjust to denounce intemperance—by way of a contrast between the new reformers and the old. The new reformers convince unregenerated drunkards that they are friends and equals—by being so. They do not refrain from denunciation out of a tactical motive but "out of the abundance of their hearts, their tongues give utterance."[44] To attribute the success of the new reformers to their disposition rather than to their tactical prudence means that the old reformers failed because of tactical ignorance and a defect of character. Formerly drink was "recognized by every body, used by every body, and repudiated by nobody,"[45] and was a respectable article of commerce. According to the older view, the victims of drink were to be pitied as unfortunate but not to be regarded as criminal or even disgraceful because drunkenness results from the abuse of a good thing and not from a bad thing. Lincoln notes that the success of the argument in favor of the existence of an overruling providence rests mainly on the same basis, the universal sense of mankind. If men do a bad thing because they take their beliefs from universal opinion, they are not necessarily bad. Their action, though bad considered in itself, springs not from a vicious or a corrupt character, but at most from a weak one. Its very weakness suggests that it should follow public opinion rather than try to find its way alone. Since most men are not entirely rational, their rationality needs the support of habit. If the attack of the old reformers on drunkenness in the name of rationality should succeed, reason itself would be destroyed because the supports necessary for its general effectiveness would be removed. The old reformers' attack on drunkenness is not merely an attack on a bad habit, but an attack on *all* habit in the name of reason.

The true task of reform, Lincoln implies, is to reform the universal sense of mankind. That cannot be accomplished by aristocratic denunciation, as we have seen, nor by the threat of punishment after death. Lincoln tells an Irish joke to illustrate the ineffectiveness of threats of evil a long way off. The threat must be present. It cannot come from those whose interest differ but must come from the people themselves, and must be found through their own experience.

Prudence and Purity

Our conclusion is strengthened by Lincoln's second argument concerning the justice of the old reformers' attitude. They fall into another error, he says, by considering all habitual drunkards to be incorrigible:

> There is in this something so repugnant to humanity, so uncharitable, so cold-blooded and feelingless, that it never did, nor ever can enlist the enthusiasm of a popular cause. . . . We could not love the man who taught it—we could not hear him with patience. The heart could not throw open its portals to it. The generous man could not adopt it. It could not mix with his

blood. It looked so fiendishly selfish, so like throwing fathers and brothers overboard, to lighten the boat for our security—that the noble minded shrank from the manifest meanness of the thing.[46]

This seems to contradict Lincoln's plea that friendship is necessary to reform another man and that one should be tolerant of weakness. If we are to become friends of drunkards, ought we not also to become friends of the old reformers in order to soften them?

It now becomes clear that the counsel of friendship is not merely expediential, but that it is just to be a friend to drunkards. The old reformers neglected friendship for the sake of their own purity; they sought to throw the unregenerated overboard so as not to contaminate themselves. The theorizers Lincoln condemns are those like the old reformers who put doctrine above friendship. The logic and eloquence of the new reformers stems from their fellow-suffering with drunkards. This sympathy may be just because it may be directed to the generous sentiments gone astray in drunkards. The old reformers, on the other hand, broke the bonds between themselves and the rest of mankind by seeking to cast aside drunkards for the sake of their own purity. By rejecting man's democratic nature, they reject the foundation of justice. The intemperance of the old reformers was worse than that of the drunkards.

The Injustice of Temperance Reform

Lincoln's third and final argument concerning the injustice of the old reformers reveals that their aims are not simply to reform others. Rather their actions were done in order that "the grace of temperance might abound to the temperate *then*, and to all mankind some hundred years *thereafter*."[47] The real concern of the old reformers was their own salvation, to be gained by destroying or casting aside all the evil that threatened to contaminate them. If this attempt made hell of the present, it was justified by the purified world that would result "some hundred years thereafter." "Great distance, in either time or space, has wonderful power to lull and render quiescent the human mind."[48] What can the future state of perfection mean to someone who is never going to see it? In working for future good, the old reformers neglect the good of those now living.

The Washingtonians do not fall into these errors. They deny that any man is incorrigible. They work for the present as well as the future, extending hope to all. They prove the truth of their position by their success. Lincoln reverses his earlier implication. Previously he had attributed sincere friendship to the new reformers, although he needed only to argue that they *acted* as friends to show that they have the correct method of reform. Now he attributes only charitable *actions* to the Washingtonians, although he should show that they act *sincerely* if he is to prove that they are indeed just. The new reformers at least act charitably, however, in that they do not denounce those who do not deserve to be denounced. If they err, it is by attributing more to their subjects than their subjects deserve. This cannot be harmful to the drunkards because, if they are incorrigible, there is nothing that may be done about it, and if they are not, something may indeed be done. It is a safe, if not entirely true, opinion)

Democrats cannot be molded or reformed by oligarchs or aristocrats, but must rise through those who were once humbled. Lincoln's rise from log cabin to white house must be the psychic path of every democratic leader)

Self-Government and the Principle of Equality

Is the principle that all men are created equal a moral principle? At first glance, the answer seems obvious. It is not a moral principle, but, as Jefferson says, a self-evident truth. It concerns not what is good and bad, but what is true and false. It is related to morality; it is the truth that establishes the limits of morality, or that establishes the context within which there is morality. Actions of men in conformity with this truth are moral. Actions that constitute a practical denial of this truth—such as slavery—are immoral. It is, as Lincoln says, not a moral principle but the "father of all moral principle."

But fathers are related to sons. It is not simply a statement of what is true and false. It is *peculiarly* related to moral principles. To change one's opinion regarding the truth or falsity of this principle is to change one's political morals. Hence it is not a morally indifferent matter whether one believes all men are created equal or not. Failure to believe this principle is a moral as well as an intellectual failure. Recognizing this, Lincoln refers to the principle as a "moral sentiment."

Prudence, too, is a combination of truth and virtue. The aim of prudence is right action. Right action will result if one has the right disposition plus knowledge of how that disposition should display itself in a particular action. Practical knowledge is at the service of good character. But in the case of the Declaration's great principle, we have a combination of a disposition of character and a truth of theory, not of practice. The truth involved is not a truth for guiding right disposition into right action in particular circumstances, but is a self-evident and universal truth, disdaining particulars.

Now, whether one considers belief in the principle to be a virtue or not, practical problems result. If it is a virtue, it is a virtue as an absolute and universal truth, and not only this, but it is the foundation of all other virtues. Men would not merely be immoral for failing to believe that all men are created equal, but they could not be good at all: they would be evil at the core of their being. This removes vital questions from the sphere of prudence. Certain abolitionists are perhaps the extreme example of this kind of Americanism in Lincoln's time. Since "all men are created equal" is a moral truth of the kind mentioned, those who deny that equality are the incarnation of evil. There can be no toleration of slavery, even momentarily, no matter what the consequences of trying to abolish it immediately, because it is not a question properly dealt with by the sphere of prudence. Just as there can be no justification for acting even momentarily against God, because God is the source of all goodness, so there can be no justification for acquiescing in any practical denial of equality. Necessity is no argument against God, neither would it be any argument against equality.

On the other hand, if it is not a moral virtue to believe that all men are created equal, to deny its truth is not immoral. The nature of immorality is determined by the consent of the governed. But there is no moral limit to consent if equality is not a principle of morality. If men consent to deny the principle of equality, that is not a moral failing, however much it may deny the truth. To put it another way, men owe no duties to those outside the political community. If the negro is not a part of the political community, as he was not before the Civil War, one does not have any moral obligation to grant him the equality that truth would give. It is a matter of moral indifference whether slavery is voted up or down. Consent, or public opinion, determines what is moral. It would seem that the difficulty is resolvable on Jeffersonian grounds only if this truth is self-evident in the sense of being evident to all men, for then public opinion would coincide with morality. But Lincoln denies that it is self-evident in this way: if it were, it would not need public support.)

The principle of popular morality thus both seems necessary to popular government and, at the same time, creates difficulties threatening to destroy self-government. Democracy seems to devour itself. It is either too inflexible or too flexible. It leads either to an absolute virtue disdaining prudence or to an expediency without regard to virtue. Yet Lincoln rejects all suggestions of tempering democracy through an admixture of aristocratic restraint. We must see how Lincoln proposes to moderate the excesses of democracy. He suggests that the American people must indeed become God's chosen people.)

IV.

THE GETTYSBURG ADDRESS
AND SACRED POLITICS

Four score and seven years ago our fathers brought forth on this continent, a new nation, conceived in liberty, and dedicated to the proposition that all men are created equal.

Now we are engaged in a great civil war, testing whether that nation, or any nation so conceived and so dedicated, can long endure. We are met on a great battle-field of that war. We have come to dedicate a portion of that field, as a final resting place for those who here gave their lives that the nation might live. It is altogether fitting and proper that we should do this.

But in a larger sense, we can not dedicate—we can not consecrate—we can not hallow—this ground. The brave men, living and dead, who struggled here, have consecrated it, far above our poor power to add or detract. The world will little note, nor long remember what we say here, but it can never forget what they did here. It is for us the living, rather, to be dedicated here to the unfinished work which they who fought here have thus far so nobly advanced. It is rather for us to be here dedicated to the great task remaining before us—that from these honored dead we take increased devotion to that cause for which they gave the last full measure of devotion—that we here highly resolve that these dead shall not have died in vain—that this nation, under God, shall have a new birth of freedom—and that government of the people, by the people, for the people, shall not perish from the earth.

* * *

But [the Gettysburg Address] is more than an admirable piece of English composition, it is an amazingly comprehensive and forceful presentation of the principles for which the war then was waging. . . . Above all it was a declaration of America's fundamental principles. It truthfully represented the spirit of that for which men fought, not only at Gettysburg but at Runnymeade, at Bunker Hill, and on the plains of Flanders.[1]

Lincoln's countrymen have long shared the opinion of Lord Curzon that the Gettysburg Address expresses the fundamental principles and spirit of America. Whether with the grudging caution of Longfellow's, "Seems to me, admirable," or the uninhibited boldness of "Besides the Sermon on the Mount, in human appreciation, has been placed Lincoln's speech at Gettysburg,"[2] Americans have celebrated the words spoken at Gettysburg. In so doing they have frequently celebrated themselves, for this venerated speech in turn venerates America. America is infused with a universal and decisive mission. What is done here by one nation will determine whether "any nation so conceived and so dedicated can long endure." The great question of whether "government of the people, by the people, for the people" shall perish from the earth rests upon the resolve of this one people. The Gettysburg Address charges the American nation with a task that makes its continued existence crucial for all mankind.

The conviction that America has a special mission was not new with Lincoln, but the passion which he breathed into an old theme can be seen by comparing his words with an analogous passage from the *Federalist Papers*. First, the observations of Hamilton:

It has frequently been remarked that it seems to have been reserved to the people of this country, by their conduct and example, to decide the important question, whether societies of men are really capable or not, of establishing good government from reflection and choice, or whether they are forever destined to depend for their political constitutions, on accident and force.[3]

Now the words of Lincoln:

Fourscore and seven years ago our fathers brought forth on this continent a new nation, conceived in liberty, and dedicated to the proposition that all men are created equal.

Now we are engaged in a great civil war, testing whether that nation, or any nation so conceived and so dedicated, can long endure.)

/But there is more to the Gettysburg Address than an old theme newly impassioned. We have shown in the second chapter that Lincoln thought the bonds uniting men to their country were weakening in the years before the Civil War)/This was in part because passions that had been directed against Great Britain during the Revolution were now turned inward)/More important, the bonds were weakening because they had been improperly made. The work of the Founders was defective in that it relied upon, and fostered, passions which, however useful and necessary in the short run, in the long run were destructive of the unity and principles of the republic)/The conclusion of that analysis was not merely that the old principles had to be newly impassioned, but that the old principles themselves were in part responsible for the threat to the country. One could not remedy the danger by simply infusing passion into the old principles)

/This analysis is not repudiated by the Gettysburg Address. In fact the Address brings to flower the seeds which Lincoln had sown more than a quarter century earlier. At the same time that it infuses American politics with a crucial mission for all men, it reveals an almost frightening detachment from the traditional understanding of that mission. In apparently repeating the principles of the Declaration of Independence, Lincoln subtly changes their meaning. He reveals the difficulties inherent in the original principles and seeks to resolve them. It is surely one of the wonders of our history that the most authoritative expression of American democracy is also a most penetrating scrutiny of its dilemmas. In the Gettysburg Address Lincoln wrought the change which he could but advise in the Lyceum Speech.>

/Many have read the Address without realizing how problematic are its assertions or how detached its author. This is not accidental. Its simplicity and clarity make it seem unproblematic. Furthermore, the speech has moved Lincoln's countrymen in part because the language is familiar to them and is indeed their own.[4] That this is a new nation unlike the old ones of Europe, that all men are created equal, that this nation seeks freedom, that the government is based

on the people, are ideas as commonplace as they are vital, from the
origins of the country to the present. It is not surprising that those
who seek the literary origins and analogies of the Address have
found that nearly every phrase in it had previously been uttered by
some other American.[5]

But the simplicity of the speech does not stem from its unproblematic character nor its clarity from the use of customary and
familiar words. Many have used the language while few have been
so moving or so clear. To use the customary language not only
without appearing to be customary, but with power, is an achievement which those who doubt its difficulty should try to duplicate.
The language is indeed that used by every American politician since
Jefferson. It is the structure of the speech that reveals Lincoln's
detachment from the traditional meaning of the language. One
cannot properly study the words or phrases of the Address without
also studying its structure. Only then will its unique character be
seen and understood. Many American statesmen, we repeat, have
used the language. Some American statesmen have been detached
in various ways from its traditional meaning.[6] But in none is such a
profound detachment combined with such a noted defense of the
tradition as in Lincoln's speech at Gettysburg. Lincoln alone seems
to have come, in the full Biblical meaning of the phrase, not to
destroy the law but to fulfill it.

Religious or Humanistic?

Many readers have sensed that the Gettysburg Address goes
deeper than an unquestioning sympathy for democracy. Frequently
they have tried to force the Address to reveal its meaning by asking
it preconceived questions, rather than by letting questions arise out
of problems in the text. If parts are torn out of context, they may
reveal some wondrous things which the speech does not contain or
contains only in a qualified sense. A subtle speech, like a subtle
man, must first be heard before it can be questioned.

If one begins with the preconceived question, "Is this speech
religious or humanistic?," one arrives at conflicting conclusions.
The trouble is that the question seeks to understand the subtlety of
the Address in terms of an unsubtle distinction between "religious"
and "humanistic." Nevertheless it will be fruitful to look briefly at

two authors who ask this question, if only to avoid their pitfalls. Florence Jeanne Goodman's essay argues that Lincoln used Pericles' funeral oration from Thucydides as his model; William J. Wolf's book, that the deeper meaning of the speech stems from its latent Christianity.[7]

Mrs. Goodman reflects on the fact that the two words, "under God," were not present in the written text Lincoln had on the platform at Gettysburg, but were added during the speech. She finds this circumstance to be especially significant because of the care with which the Address is written. The last sentence, into which the words were inserted, is a particularly concentrated expression of Lincoln's thought. According to Mrs. Goodman, these words were left out of the original draft for two reasons. First, "In societies which are predominantly humanist in their practice, even though religion exists, the name of God is not always in the mouth of the people or their leaders."[8] Second, although Lincoln was not an atheist, he did not share the superstitions of the many. In fact, he was closely following Pericles' humanist oration, in which there is no mention of the gods. Lincoln, no more than Pericles, shared the religious beliefs of the people. Hence he held out hope of fame for the dead as did Pericles, without noticing that he had not held out hope of heaven. "Not until he had almost finished speaking, did it occur to him to mention God, and then he smoothly slipped in the saving phrase, between the two parts of a future tense verb, and the common people's feelings were spared."[9]

Wolf believes the phrase was an "inspired addition."[10] He argues that, far from being humanistic, the Gettysburg Address reveals Lincoln's deepened sense of consecration at the time, and he finds affinities both of style and thought to the Bible and Christianity. Although there are no quotations from the Bible in the speech, the language is Biblical and has the cadences of the King James version. For example, "Four score and seven years ago" is "an inspired adaptation of Old Testament counting."[11] More significantly the central image in the speech is the rite of baptism or the solemn dedication of children to God:

> The New Testament describes baptism as a dying to sin with Christ in his death and as a rising to newness of life in the power of his resurrection. Lincoln conflates the themes of the life of man

in birth, baptismal dedication, and spiritual rebirth with the experience of the nation in its eighty-seven years of history.

Although founded on the proposition that all men are created equal, the nation had denied its universal dedication by narrowing "all" to "all white men." At Gettysburg the old man of sin died that the nation might be reborn in the truth of a growing democracy for all men everywhere.[12]

Furthermore, to see the Civil War as a test is also a religious interpretation. While the verb, "testing," stems in part from Euclid, it:

> . . . takes on the overtones of a test of faith such as Abraham's or Job's in the Old Testament. . . . Lincoln's way of rooting democracy in the will of God made it a dynamic faith to live by. The Civil War was a "test" or "trial" of that faith. The theme of being justified by faith, an echo of the Puritan religious heritage, is also in the background of this language about the testing of a proposition.[13]

Wolf finds the speech to be religious in both style and substance.

Both of these interpretations are doubtful, although not equally. Mrs. Goodman's argument does not hold. Perhaps humanist societies often do not speak of God. This generality, however, does not explain why Lincoln would not mention God in this particular speech. It would be hard to establish a general rule that American politicians have refrained from invoking God. Further, this was not any occasion, but the solemn dedication of a cemetery for those who had fallen in what was then the bloodiest battle of modern warfare. It is safe to say that on such an occasion, even if the United States of 1863 be considered a humanist society, the mention of God would be the rule rather than the exception. In the speech preceeding Lincoln's at Gettysburg, Edward Everett mentions God in the first sentence and in several contexts thereafter. This is not due to his unusual piety. In fact his speech clearly looks back to the Athens of Pericles and not to Jerusalem. Everett begins by drawing a lengthy parallel between Pericles' situation and his own, casting the minds of his audience back to Greece and inviting them to compare his speech to Pericles'. It ends by quoting and affirming a judgment of Pericles that reveals (as does his whole speech) that Everett was quite unconcerned with the fate of the dead in the next world.[14] What is surprising is not Lincoln's mention of God but Pericles' failure to mention the gods.

Mrs. Goodman's second argument that Lincoln was following Pericles and he put in the phrase while speaking to avoid injuring the feelings of the common people is weak. If the Address was prepared with meticulous care, as Mrs. Goodman rightly argues, it is difficult to suppose that offering the hope of heaven did not occur to Lincoln before he reached the platform. It implies he was following Pericles blindly. This is in contradiction with her main argument, which is ". . . not only that Lincoln consulted the Greek master but that he surpassed him."[15]

Mrs. Goodman should show whether or not the phrase is extraneous to the thought of the speech; it matters little at what point the phrase was inserted or whether humanist societies generally speak about God. From the mere fact that it was inserted on the platform, one is equally entitled to assume that it was put in to salve the feelings of the people or that it was "inspired." Nor does it help to assume that Lincoln followed the customs of humanist societies; it would have to be proven. Finally, it is a mistake to argue from the Address's supposed model, even if the model were known. In fact, it is only conjectured. To make conjectures about the antecedents of the Address may help reveal its meaning, but only on condition that the conjectures find support within the Address itself. Otherwise one is guilty of appealing from the better known to the less known, and of blurring the differences which may exist between the Address and its supposed model.

On his side, Mr. Wolf argues that partial similarities suffice to prove total similarity. The similarities of language and style to the Bible by themselves prove nothing about the religious qualities of Lincoln's speech. Because "four score and seven years ago" is an adaptation of a Biblical method of counting, it does not follow that this method is *necessarily* religious. Rather than proving Wolf's point, the image of baptism in the speech casts doubt upon it. Is it justified, in a Christian or "inspired" speech, to apply terms which originally refer to events in the salvation of an individual to the salvation of a nation? Wolf's conclusion that "at Gettysburg the old man of sin died that the nation might be reborn in the truth of a growing democracy for all men everywhere" demonstrates the difficulties which vitiate his interpretation. One might question whether this statement accurately represents Lincoln's view of what happened at Gettysburg. But in any case, it is hardly true Christianity, and certainly not orthodox Christianity, that could interpret the new life after rebirth from sin to be the "truth of a growing democracy for all men everywhere." Wolf can consider the imagery to be unambiguously Christian only by ignoring the content of the images.

Both Mr. Wolf and Mrs. Goodman err by trying to interpret parts of the speech outside their context in the whole. Neither the phrase "under God" nor the image of birth, baptism, and rebirth can be properly seen if isolated. By isolating these parts each is able to find in past traditions the source of the profundity which he senses in the speech. Mrs. Goodman finds the Address to be the culmination of two thousand years of humanistic funeral orations; Mr. Wolf finds it to be a magnificent restatement of the Christian creed. Yet the parts to which each points are found in the same speech. The "humanist" concerns and the "religious" imagery are united; yet in neither Mr. Wolf's nor Mrs. Goodman's interpretation could they be, for "humanist" and "religious" are opposites. From the viewpoint of either tradition, the Address is contradictory; and from one it is possibly blasphemous. But it may be that its contradictions arise from viewing the Address in the light of tradition, not from the Address itself. In other words, the Address may be something other or something more than a repetition of traditional beliefs. To see whether this is so we must begin from the Address itself; we cannot begin from a model or a tradition.

Principle and History

The Gettysburg Address consists of three paragraphs. The first paragraph tells the story of the nation's past; the second places the Civil War and dedication of the Gettysburg cemetery within the context of that story. The third paragraph may be divided into two parts. The first three sentences argue that dedication of the cemetery is inadequate because it is inferior to the consecration performed by the soliders on the battlefield. The rest of the speech seeks to delineate and inspire the audience to a more adequate dedication. The speech may thus be regarded as having four sections. It moves from the past in the first section, to the present action in the central sections, to the future action required in the final section.[16]

The first paragraph tells the story of the nation's past. It recalls the actions of the Founders and restates their principles. It invites close comparison with the Declaration of Independence by using similar language as well as an explicit reference to the date of its composition. Jefferson wrote:

> We hold these truths to be self-evident, that all men are created equal, that they are endowed by their Creator with certain un-alienable Rights, that among these are Life, Liberty and the pursuit of Happiness. — That to secure these rights, Governments are instituted among Men, deriving their just powers from the consent of the governed, —

In recalling this original act, Lincoln says:

> Four score and seven years ago our fathers brought forth on this continent, a new nation, conceived in liberty, and dedicated to the proposition that all men are created equal.

Lincoln both tells the story of the nation's founding and reasserts the principles of its Founders. The major problem of the first paragraph arises from the tension between telling that story and reasserting the Declaration's principles.

If we view the Declaration in its own terms, we are forced to say that it is unnecessary to tell the story of the founding in order to see the truth of its principles, although the story is necessary to under-stand the Founders' actions. The Declaration asserts its principles to be self-evident truths, meant to apply to all men everywhere. No particular circumstances could add or detract from them. The Gettysburg Address, however, connects these principles to the nation founded by "our fathers." This connection does not make the principles truer; they are true whether or nor our fathers held them.

Not only does it not affect the truth of the principles, but the story of the founding provides no reason for holding the principles dearer. According to the Declaration, we hold to these principles because they are true, not because they are ours. We resort to these principles, to be sure, because of the suffering and injustice we have undergone. The Declaration holds before our eyes the tyranny of

George III and the patience of the Americans to show that its principles apply in these particuar circumstances, but the principles stand independently of circumstance. The Declaration does not look back to our peculiar customs to justify its principles, but appeals only to the "laws of Nature and of Nature's God." We stand on the truth because it is the truth.)

By telling the story of the founding despite its irrelevance to either the truth of the Declaration's principles or the reasons for adhering to them, Lincoln seems to be departing from the Declaration. He suggests either that we hold to the principles because they were held by our fathers, or that the truth itself is in question because it rests upon the authority of our fathers, or both. Although Lincoln believes that equality applies to all men everywhere, he points not to a natural but to a customary origin of the principle. To place the principles of the Declaration within the story of their embodiment in a nation brough forth by our fathers is not a simple addition. It implies a change in the status of the principles. In reasserting the principles of the Declaration, Lincoln questions their original understanding. We must examine with care the modifications he makes)

Self-Evident Truth or Proposition?

The changes that Lincoln makes in the Declaration's principles can be approached by examining the most obvious similarity of the Declaration to the Address. Like the Declaration, the Gettysburg Address asserts that all men are created equal. However, Lincoln terms this assertion a proposition; the Declaration claims it is a self-evident truth. The geometric language used by both Jefferson and Lincoln clarifies the distinction. A self-evident truth is necessarily true and does not need to be proven; a proposition may be either true or false and must be proven to be one or the other.)

A proposition may be either true or false, while a self-evident truth can only be true. When Senator Sumner first read the Address, he thought the word, "proposition," was inappropriately used.[17] We may surmise that he thought it inappropriate precisely for the shadow of doubt it seems to cast on the principle that was undoubted in the Declaration. Yet it is hard to believe that Lincoln did not realize the implication of his change, or that he used the word only because he could not think of a better. The better word, if he did not want to suggest doubt, was available to him from the Declaration; he could have said, ". . . dedicated to the *truth* that all men are created equal. . . ." That he changed the term, while borrowing still from geometry, indicates that he knew what he said.

The change from "truth" to "proposition" does not merely cast doubt on the truth of the principle, but changes its entire status. The Declaration claims that the truth that all men are created equal is self-evident. By this, the Declaration does not mean that this truth is readily apparent to everyone. Clearly Jefferson knew that there were many people who did not assent to the principle. Rather the Declaration means that the principle contains within itself the evidence of its own validity. Its predicate is contained within its subject. If one understands what the term "men" means, one knows that all men are created equal. To those who grasp the meaning of the terms, the truth is "self-evident." Thus the truth of this principle is not found by a chain of reasoning, but is rather the point from which reasoning must begin. One grasps that all men are created equal; one may then reason to the conclusion that the just powers of government derive from the consent of the governed.

Yet at Gettysburg Lincoln changes this status. As every student of geometry knows, a proposition refers to a theorem or problem. In either case it can be known to be true only by reference to a higher principle. It does not contain internally the evidence of its own validity; it must be proven true. The self-evident truth of the Declaration thus becomes, in the Address, a proposition which must be shown to be true by reference to another principle. Then this truth is no longer seen as the beginning of political wisdom. The axiom from which all other political principles are derived is itself dependent on higher principles.

Lincoln was well aware of the status of the principles of the Declaration. As he once explained:

> But soberly, it is now no child's play to save the principles of Jefferson from total overthrow in this nation.
>
> One would start with great confidence that he could convince any sane child that the simpler propositions of Euclid are true; but, nevertheless, he would fail, utterly, with one who should deny the definitions and axioms. The principles of Jefferson are the definitions and axioms of free society. And yet they are denied, and evaded, with no small show of success.[19]

But the quotation also reveals that Lincoln thought the status of the principles presented a problem.

As indicated, the term "self-evident" has two meanings. A principle may be self-evident in itself, having its predicate contained in its subject, or it may be self-evident for us, being obvious to us. The Declaration asserts that the principle that all men are created equal is self-evident in itself. However, the Declaration is ambiguous. It is not clear that it does not also mean that the principle is self-evident for us. The ambiguity is not trivial. One of the truths maintained by the Declaration is that "governments derive their just powers from the consent of the governed." This creates a difficulty. If governments should be founded on self-evident truths and yet derive their powers from the governed, then either the governed must consent to the self-evident truths or the two principles are incompatible. What happens if the governed should not consent to the proposition that all men are created equal? If the governed are expected to consent to the self-evident truths, then these truths must be knowable to the governed as well as in themselves.

The quotation from Lincoln reveals the depth of the difficulty. A self-evident principle is not teachable in the normal sense. One can prove a proposition in geometry if it is denied, but one cannot prove an axiom. If someone denies the axioms of the Declaration, there is no way to teach him by reasoning that they are indeed true. Hence the success of the project of founding the country on self-evident truths depends upon these truths becoming self-evident not only in themselves but also for us—in the sense that they are obvious to everyone. The two meanings of the term "self-evident" are not clearly distinguished in the Declaration because the Declaration must implicitly assert their practical identity.

The problem thus disguised by the Declaration became increasingly acute before the Civil War. What happens if the axioms do not become obvious for everyone? Indeed, what if they are denied "with no small show of success?" How can one re-establish those axioms when they are not teachable? Certainly it would then be "no child's play to save the principles of Jefferson from total overthrow in this nation." The Declaration presupposes an identity it provides no means to secure.

Now Jefferson knew that the axiom of the Declaration was not self-evident to all; he knew that men must be instructed (in the broad sense of the term) in its meaning. But Jefferson thought that there were natural aristoi from whom enlightenment could flow to men in general, provided the aristoi themselves were properly educated and properly checked to prevent their tendency to serve their own ambition instead of the people.[20] But for Lincoln, who denied that there were any such men except for rare geniuses, the Declaration's identity could not be assumed through a balance of natural aristocrats and people.

The problem, as Lincoln saw it, is solvable in principle only if it is possible to convert the axioms of the Declaration into propositions. Only if one can find a higher principle from which to prove that all men are created equal is it possible to re-establish the great principle of the Declaration. Then only does it become teachable. But it is no mean feat to accomplish this transformation, for how can the point from which reasoning must begin become merely a link in the chain of reasoning. Furthermore this transformation in itself is not enough. One must not only find a higher truth; one must find a higher truth that will gain the consent of the people. Then one must reason from it to convince them that all men are created equal.

The Gettysburg Address is primarily concerned with the question of whether a nation founded on the principles of Declaration can long endure. Since time has shown that the great self-evident principle of the Declaration is not self-evident for us, the answer to the question depends on whether it is possible to teach the principle. The Declaration's answer is "no, it is not possible." The answer to the question, therefore, cannot be unequivocally "yes." It can be "yes" only if it is possible to convert the self-evident truth of the Declaration into a proposition that is teachable. But then the principle is changed. One cannot regenerate the Declaration without changing its meaning.

From Beginning to End

The Gettysburg Address is not primarily concerned with the question of whether the proposition to which the country is dedicated is true. Its primary concern is rather the question, we repeat, of whether a nation so dedicated can long endure. One does not answer the second question by answering the first: Even if the proposition is true, it may not be possible to found a country upon it. It must not only be true, but it must be known to be true, or believed to be true, by the people. We have said that the self-evident truth must be a proposition if it is to be teachable. This is not strictly true. It need not be a proposition; it might be a teachable truth. Lincoln could have simply dropped "self-evident" from the terminology of the Declaration, leaving "truth." By changing the term to "proposition" Lincoln suggests a doubt about whether the proposition is true—a doubt he would not need to suggest. Hence our explanation for the change in terminology is not sufficient.

The additional problem calling forth the new terminology can be seen by asking whether it would be possible to found a country on a truth which is not self-evident. The answer is that it would not be possible in the sense in which the Declaration conceives it possible to found a country on a self-evident truth. The Declaration says that governments are founded on certain self-evident truths. As we have pointed out, this means that these truths—and in particular the truth that all men are created equal—are the axioms of politics. All other political principles are derived from them. If, however, the originating principle is not a self-evident truth, but a truth derived from a higher truth, how is it possible to found a nation upon it? If it is not the most fundamental truth, should one not try to substitute the more fundamental principle for the derived one? After all, there may be cases not covered by the lesser principle, but only by the more comprehensive one. To admit that one's principles are not the most fundamental seems an open invitation to revolution. If the principle is not the whole truth, it ought to be discarded for the whole truth. Otherwise one cannot be sure that the foundation is secure. To convert the principle of the Declaration into a derived truth may make it teachable; but then it becomes impossible to found a country upon it.

If the principle is a proposition, however, this difficulty is solved by changing the sense in which the country is founded on the principle. The essence of a proposition is that it has to be proven. To found a nation on a proposition is thus to commit the nation to proving the proposition true. The principle becomes the end or goal towards which the country must move, rather than the beginning from which all other political principles are derived. What, for Jefferson, was a truth upon which all else is to be built becomes, for Lincoln, a proposition which one must prove. The goal of the country is to prove the proposition true. Instead of a foundation upon which one builds, the principle becomes the building one seeks to construct.)

This distinction becomes clearer when we see the contrasting conceptions held by the Declaration and the Address of how the principle is related to the nation. Jefferson said, "We *hold* these truths to be self-evident . . ." Lincoln says that the nation is "*dedicated* to the proposition . . ." To hold something means to have a grasp upon it, to have it. As we have seen, the Declaration contemplates just such a grasping of its first principles. To be dedicated to something means that one does not have it in hand; one is devoted to something, a person or purpose. One surrenders oneself to something else. A dedication implies that the goal to which one is dedicated is not yet reached. To hold a truth, on the other hand, means that one already has it. The principle which is the point of departure for politics in the Declaration becomes the end to which politics is dedicated in the Address.)

Now, to be dedicated to a proposition is to be dedicated to proving it. The actions of this country are aimed at proving the proposition true. The proposition is to be proven by action! But then the proposition may be the highest political *principle*. It is transcended not by another principle, but by the actions of this nation.)

But how can one prove a principle by action? We have shown in the previous chapter that Lincoln considered the proposition that all men are created equal to be the foundation of popular morality. However, this did not mean that men automatically follow this principle. To be effective this principle has to be embodied in a nation and gain the weight of public opinion. Men will recognize it as the foundation of their own morality, but only with the guidance of public opinion. The principle, then, is the guide and standard for public opinion; but, in turn, the principle depends upon public opinion for its effectiveness. This same relationship exists in the Gettysburg Address in regard to men's actions. The proposition, as the end to which the country is dedicated, is the guide for the actions of the nation dedicated to it: that nation is to seek to prove the proposition true. Since the principle, however, is seen to be true only after it is established, it can be proved only by being put into effect. It is taught by practicing it. It is proved by action.)

We must reiterate that Lincoln is asking the question, How can a nation be founded on the principle that all men are created equal? He is not asking the question, "Is the principle true?" Hence Lincoln's change of the principle from a self-evident truth to a proposition is not directed to the question of the truth of the principle; it is rather changed in order to solve the problem of how a nation may be founded on the principle. In other words, the principle is a proposition not from the viewpoint of some neutral observer testing its truth, but from the viewpoint of the nation committed to it. It was the mistake of the Declaration to identify these two viewpoints. The Declaration identified the two because it maintained that a nation could be founded on self-evident truths. Lincoln shows that it cannot; hence the two viewpoints are distinct. The principle is a proposition which must be proved by action *for* this nation, or any nation.

The nation, then, must be founded on belief. One must be dedicated to the proposition. Because the principle is the end or goal of the country, it is not yet ours. We have not yet shown that all men are created equal. But how can we be dedicated to a principle which we do not know to be true? May not our dedication be misplaced? The principle that all men are created equal, because it is not known to be true, requires testimony to be believed.

Rights and Liberty

That the nation was conceived in liberty is presumption that its dedication was justified. The change we have seen in the meaning of equality is rivaled by the change in liberty. The Declaration explains in what sense all men are created equal by saying that they "are endowed by their Creator with certain unalienable Rights, that among these are Life, Liberty, and the Pursuit of Happiness." "Liberty" in the Declaration is either one of the unalienable rights that all men have, or the sum of all unalienable rights. In the Address "liberty" describes the action by which the nation was conceived. Instead of a right, liberty becomes the state of those who acted. It describes the men who conceived the nation.

The startling fact is that Lincoln suggests that our fathers were free before the right of liberty was guaranteed. They conceived the nation in liberty before the nation was brought forth as the guarantee of the right of liberty. Freedom is not dependent upon men's rights being secured. Our fathers were free before their rights were secured. (This is not to say that to have those rights secured may not be a highly useful step towards achieving this freedom in practice.) Now one may have his right to liberty secured without being free. That is, according to the understanding implicit in the Declaration, a state cannot force a man to be free. Precisely because he is forced, he is not free. Rather a state may only provide the conditions in which he may be free, if he so chooses. These conditions are rights. The job of government is to secure these conditions or rights. In the Gettysburg Address, however, Lincoln is not concerned with the right of liberty, or with these minimum conditions which allow one to be free, but with the substance of freedom. Not the right, but the exercise of freedom is Lincoln's concern. As with the principle that all men are created equal, liberty is reinterpreted to mean not the minimum conditions for freedom but the perfection of freedom.

Unlike equality, however, liberty is not the goal or end of the country. In fact, Lincoln says that our fathers once possessed it. We have not yet proved that all men are created equal, but liberty we have had. The liberty actually possessed and exercised by our fathers is part of the assurance that dedication to equality is not misplaced. Our fathers were not forced to dedicate the country to equality; they freely chose to so dedicate it. The conception is a testimony to the conceived. It does not prove the nation to be good, but it is a presumption in its favor. The quality of the conception testifies to the quality of the result.[21]

Conviction of Things Unseen

To find assurance for the presumption that our fathers brought forth a worthy offspring is Lincoln's reason for telling the story of the nation's beginning. An understanding of this story will show that the nation's dedication is not misplaced.

Our fathers "brought forth" a new nation. Our fathers seem both responsible and not responsible for the new nation. Our fathers are responsible for the existence of the country, for they brought it forth. They also conceived it in liberty and dedicated it to the proposition that all men are created equal. Not merely its existence but its form and end are the work of our fathers. The reasons Lincoln points to this distinction can be seen when it is remembered, as we have shown in the previous chapter, that the Union is a union of principle. The truth of the principle that all men are

created equal does not depend upon our fathers. They could dedicate a nation to it; they did not create it. It exists naturally as the
foundation of popular morality. Since the nation is formed by this
principle, our fathers only brought forth the nation. To "bring
forth" a nation implies that it was there to be brought forth. Our
fathers only brought forth the nation; they did not create it.

There is another sense in which our fathers only brought forth
the nation. We have pointed out that if the nation is dedicated to a
proposition, it is dedicated to action — to proving the proposition
true. Hence the United States is in a way unformed. It is formed by
being dedicated to a proposition, but since the outcome or end of
this dedication is unseen the form of the country is in doubt at a
decisive point. It is not known whether the proposition may provide a proper foundation for the country. Whether dedication to
the proposition is good or bad is shown only by the actions of the
men who come after the Founders. The country is formed by a
question. But a country is less formed by a question, where there is
something in doubt, than it is by an undoubted principle. Although
our fathers brough forth a new nation, they turned a child loose
whose final form is not determined by them, even as a natural
father cannot determine the final form of his natural child.

Hence Lincoln shows that the nation cannot ultimately be judged
on the grounds that our fathers made it. We cannot prove its
goodness by looking to its founders. However Lincoln does seem to
imply that we might have increased grounds for adhering to the
nation because our fathers have brought it forth. We must see the
reasons for this implication.

The Founders were not "our fathers" in the literal sense that they
were the biological fathers of those present. There may have been
some sons of the founding generation among Lincoln's listeners;
they could not have been a majority. In any case Lincoln does not
say "the fathers of some of us" but "our fathers," clearly including
all his audience in "our." One might be tempted to regard the
Founders as "our fathers" in the sense that we are part of the nation
that they brought forth. Because we belong to the nation, they are
our fathers. But the Address indicates that the opposite is the case.
Because it was brought forth by our fathers, we belong to the
nation. The Gettysburg Address does not try to prove that the
Founders were our fathers; it rather wishes to show that we belong

to the nation. In what sense, then, were these men our fathers?
In the previous chapter we have indicated Lincoln's answer to
this question. The Founders are not our fathers in the flesh. They
are rather our moral fathers in a two-fold sense. An immigrant may
see that the Founders said that all men are created equal. Because
he recognizes the principle as the foundation of morality within
him, he can see his unity with those men. But they are not simply
his brothers. While the principle that all men are created equal is
the foundation of popular morality, that morality and principle are
in danger without public support. To be effective the principle
must be called forth to become the principle animating a country.
We are not only united with the Founders by our common principle
of morality, but our recognition of this common ground depends
upon the fact that our fathers brought forth a nation dedicated to
this principle. It was our fathers who made us in this crucial sense.
Because they are our fathers we belong to the nation. To recognize
these men as our fathers is equivalent in practice to recognizing the
truth that all men are created equal, that the nation is dedicated to
this proposition, and that its truth is dependent upon the nation.
We see ourselves as a part of the nation and the nation as a part
of us.
The way in which Lincoln tries to solve the problem of public
opinion can now be seen. The principle that all men are created
equal is effective only with the support of public opinion. How does
one maintain the principle when public opinion slips away from it?
The answer is that one forces men's attention away from the public
opinion of the moment to the public opinion of the Founders. The
authority of the Founders may recall the public opinion of the
moment to its moral principle. But that authority can be appealed
to only if the principles of the Declaration change, for the Declaration denies that one need hold the principle by authority. This
alerts us to the fact that Lincoln is bringing forth the past as well as
appealing to it.
Our fathers brought forth a new nation at a particular time and
place—four score and seven years ago on this continent. Or did
they? Could not one trace the nation back to, say, the New England
Puritans? or the Articles of Confederation? or the Constitution? Or
could one not even trace it back to the Middle Ages or classical
Greece? If there was something new with the Revolution, is that so

significant in comparison with all that was inherited? Lincoln's date seems arbitrary.

"Four score and seven years ago" was said to be an inspired adaptation of a Biblical method of counting, but what significance does that method have? Just as we noted that "our fathers" was a lie if considered as a statement of biology, so "four score and seven years ago" is arbitrary as a starting point if one seeks to find the roots of the present in the past. Rather than merely a long (because elevated) way of expressing eighty-seven, "four score and seven years ago" refers to something other then eighty-seven revolutions about the sun. Eighty-seven years before was, of course, the date of the Declaration. It is the length of time the nation has existed in its own consciousness. However, the nation was not recognized by Great Britain until the end of the Revolutionary War. More precisely, it is the length of time that the nation has been conscious. It is the length of time the nation has existed for itself.

But even this is not an historical fact. Could not one date the beginning of the nation from 1787 instead of 1776? By setting the date at 1776, Lincoln declares that we were formed as one people by the principles of the Declaration rather than by the laws of 1787. In so doing Lincoln declares what an American is. We are those who share a common memory back to 1776. Those who look merely to the Constitution without interpreting it in the light of the principles of 1776 do not fully belong to the nation. The nation to which Lincoln points is the nation Lincoln is creating by instilling and reviving a common memory, a memory both of an event and of a principle. This common memory is created in the present, by the Gettysburg Address above all. The story is arbitrary if taken to be a recital of events in the past. The Founders exist in the present as "our fathers."

Lincoln's view of the relationship of past and present in the American nation can be clarified by comparing it with that of John Dewey, who writes:

> The things in civilization we most prize are not of ourselves. They exist by the grace of the doings and sufferings of the continuous human community in which we are a link. Ours is the responsibility of conserving, rectifying and expanding the heritage of values we have received that those who come after us may

receive it more solid and secure, more widely accessible and more generously shared than we have received it.[22]

Dewey pictures the relationship of the present to the past as one of conserving, transmitting, rectifying and expanding the heritage of values. The past passes on a collection of values and they become our property and our responsibility. This is not the relationship in the Gettysburg Address. The past does not pass on a set of values, as a father might pass his estate to his son. The present does not simply receive the past, but that past does not exist without the present. This does not mean that the term "our fathers" as applied to people who were not our actual fathers is arbitrary, and that history is recreated at each succeeding moment. Rather it means that the past exists as past only from the viewpoint of a present. The judgment of the past, insofar as it is done by principles, depends on the proper selection of principles in the present. If those who exist now are corrupt, they will not interpret the past properly; in fact, they will not even see the past because the past is not simply something existing in external facts as a patrimony. The past is what it has been no matter how men may regard it. Nevertheless it cannot be seen by scientific observation. It can be seen as it has been only if the men of the present are alive to the past, which means that the past must exist in the present as part of themselves. When Lincoln views the past, he does not cull values from it, but recognizes the present for what it is. Lincoln's interpretation of the Civil War is not an arbitrary interpretation forced upon recalcitrant matter by a gifted poet. Rather it can be experienced as the correct interpretation because the souls of the citizens can understand themselves as the result of the past which Lincoln draws for them. They participate in the past by knowing themselves.

The existence of the nation which Lincoln seeks to defend depends upon continual dedication to the proposition to which its founders dedicated it. The reference to the founding fathers is not simply the call of a patriot, but an attempt to awaken the consciousness of the people to the principles to which the nation is dedicated; that is, to create the nation as Lincoln understands it within their own souls. Without that dedication the same nation would not exist. Its continued existence depends upon its continued dedication. The story is the assurance that the dedication is not misplaced.

The Present Test

The second paragraph places the Civil War and dedication of the Gettysburg Cemetery within the story told in the first paragraph. It is an application of the principles we have outlined. The Civil War is a test of "whether that nation, or any nation so conceived and so dedicated, can long endure." The test does indeed take on the overtones of a "test of faith" because the results depend upon the firmness of the country's dedication to a principle it does not know to be true. The War is also a test in the scientific sense: one must prove the proposition true by action.

By tying present events to the story of the nation's founding, Lincoln seeks to use the war to point to the principles of the founding. The war is a test not simply for America, but for any nation so conceived and so dedicated. The war has a meaning for all men. The resolve of this one nation will reveal whether any such nation can long endure. This is so, as we have seen, because the decline in public commitment to the principles of the nation is not due to an evil peculiar to this country. The Civil War raises the question of a general difficulty to a universal principle. Hence its result is decisive for other countries also. The death of the soldiers at Gettysburg is given meaning: Men give their lives for the nation because the nation transcends them. It is only through the nation that individuals make contact with its lofty principles, principles which turn out to be the foundation of their own morality. To lose the nation is to lose one's own morality. It is fitting that men die for their country, and it is fitting that their country dedicates a final resting place for them. All this seems to follow from the principles implied in the first paragraph.

Yet this unproblematic interpretation does not suffice for the occasion:

> But in a larger sense we cannot dedicate, we cannot consecrate, we cannot hallow this ground. The brave men, living and dead, who struggled here have consecrated it far above our poor power to add or detract. The world will little note nor long remember what we say here, but it can never forget what they did here.

Lincoln turns from "us" to the "brave men, living and dead, who struggled here." When one turns from our actions to theirs, ours pale. We cannot dedicate, consecrate, hallow this ground. Rather the brave men who struggled here have consecrated it far above our poor power to add or detract. Our actions are reduced in worth still further, until the contrast becomes that of words and deeds. We have only the power of our words, a power woefully inadequate when measured against their deeds)

As has often been pointed out, the statement that the world would little note nor long remember what was said at Gettysburg was wrong. Indeed, it was the opposite of the truth. If it were not for words, the deeds of the soldiers who died at Gettysburg would not be remembered. Their fame is dependent on words and most especially the masterful words of Lincoln. Their fame depends not on themselves so much as on those who extol them)

Why does Lincoln tell this lie? To comfort the hearers with the assurance of everlasting fame? Is that explanation sufficient? As Mrs. Goodman notes, in offering hope of fame, Lincoln neglects to mention the possibility of heaven. Yet if he is concerned merely with providing comfort for his audience, why does he not mention it also? Even if he did not believe in heaven, would it be more of a lie to promise them heaven than to promise them fame on the basis of their deeds rather than his words?)

The possibility that Lincoln believed that the deeds of those who struggled there would be remembered longer than his words must also be rejected. He was too well acquainted with words not to know their power. But if more proof is requested, one need only turn to the speech itself, where Lincoln says that we must "here highly resolve that these dead shall not have died in vain." He implies that it is possible that the dead will have died in vain. But if they merely died a vain death, why should the world remember it? The worth of their sacrifice is to be determined by the dedication of those yet living. Their deeds are not sufficient to earn their fame)

One may consider whether the deeds performed on the battlefield (by both living and dead) are not more worthy of fame than the words spoken at Gettysburg. If this were so, then perhaps Lincoln's lie is salutary, substituting what should be the case were justice done for what actually is the case. But it is not clear that the deeds of those brave men were really more worthy of remembrance than Lincoln's words)

Lincoln deprecates the power of his words because it is possible that the dead shall have died in vain. Their deaths find their worth in advancing what lies beyond them, the life of the nation dedicated to the proposition that all men are created equal. If this principle is generalized, it means not only those who died at Gettysburg but those presently living depend for the worth of their living on those who come after them. Human responsibility extends not only in the present and to the future, but to the past. In order that the dead shall not have died in vain, it is necessary that men become aware of their responsibility by becoming aware of the sacrifice of the dead. As in the first paragraph where Lincoln finds in the quality of the founding act a guarantee that belief is not misplaced, so here the sacrifice of the soldiers is used to awaken his audience to a renewed dedication.

The immortality of the dead at Gettysburg depends upon the immortality of the nation, and the immortality of the nation depends upon the immortality of its dedication to the principle that all men are created equal. The immortality of the dead depends upon the immortality of the principle for which they died. From the viewpoint of the nation (which, we repeat, is the viewpoint of the Address) the immortality of the principle depends upon the immortality of the nation.

The central contention of the final exhortation is that the nation should have a new birth of freedom. Lincoln has in mind a birth of freedom for the black man. But the context makes clear he believes in a new birth of freedom for the white man as well. The speech as a whole makes clear that Lincoln does not merely wish a return to the founding fathers. Their principles must be reinterpreted to solve the problems which we have seen, as Lincoln reinterprets the principles in the Address. Their deeds must be improved upon. We must have a rebirth of freedom, as our fathers had freedom, not to repeat their acts but to transcend them.

Government of, by, and for the People

The final phrase of the Address is perhaps the most famous: we here highly resolve "that government of the people, by the people, for the people, shall not perish from the earth." There is an old controversy concerning how Lincoln delivered the phrase. Did he emphasize the prepositions or "people?" The contention is that if he emphasized "people," this would somehow cast Lincoln's sympathies more with democracy than if he emphasized the prepositions. What is dimly perceived is the tension between the three relationships indicated by the prepositions and the fact that "the people" is one term of all three relationships. The prepositions indicate relationships between men and government. "Of the people" indicates those who are the source of the government; "by the people" those who govern; and "for the people" in whose benefit the government governs. In showing his awareness of the relationships that might give rise to undemocratic elements, while establishing the "people" as supreme in all three relationships, Lincoln makes crystal-clear his awareness of the problem and the definitiveness of his solution.

The Gettysburg Address seems to deny that politics has limits. The universal principles of the Declaration are seen to be embodied in this country, and dependent upon it. Hence the nation has a universal task decisive not only for itself but for all mankind. The present moment then comes to embody this decisiveness. The present moment is the crisis. It is decisive not only for the present and the future, but for the past. It is decisive for the dead as well as the living. If the present generation fails the test, the dead shall have died in vain. Life is not an inheritance from the dead, but the dead receive life from the living. The life of our fathers, the death of the soldiers at Gettysburg, and our rebirth of freedom all depend upon the existence of this nation. The Union becomes a sacred union, bound by belief, and sacred because it is the beginning and end of belief.

This expansion of politics, until it absorbs even the meaning of life and death, must be counterbalanced by the Second Inaugural which seems to draw limits to the possibilities of political action.

V.

THE SECOND INAUGURAL
AND THE LIMITS OF POLITICS

(At this second appearing to take the oath of the presidential office, there is less occasion for an extended address than there was at the first. Then a statement, somewhat in detail, of a course to be pursued, seemed fitting and proper. Now, at the expiration of four years, during which public declarations have been constantly called forth on every point and phase of the great contest which still absorbs the attention, and engrosses the energies of the nation, little that is new could be presented. The progress of our arms, upon which all else chiefly depends, is as well known to the public as to myself; and it is, I trust, reasonably satisfactory and encouraging to all. With high hope for the future, no prediction in regard to it is ventured.

On the occasion corresponding to this four years ago, all thoughts were anxiously directed to an impending civil war. All dreaded it—all sought to avert it. While the inaugural address was being delivered from this place, devoted altogether to *saving* the Union without war, insurgent agents were in the city seeking to *destroy* it without war—seeking to dissolve the Union, and divide effects, by negotiation. Both parties deprecated war; but one of them would *make* war rather than let the nation survive; and the other would *accept* war rather than let it perish. And the war came.

One eighth of the whole population were colored slaves, not distributed generally over the Union, but localized in the Southern part of it. These slaves constituted a peculiar and powerful interest. All knew that this interest was, somehow, the cause of the war. To strengthen, perpetuate, and extend this interest was the object for which the insurgents would rend the Union, even by war, while the government claimed no right to do more than to restrict the territorial enlargement of it. Neither party expected for the war, the magnitude, or the duration, which it has already attained. Neither anticipated that the *cause* of the conflict might cease with, or even before, the conflict itself should cease. Each looked for an easier triumph, and a result less fundamental and astounding. Both read the same Bible, and pray to the same God; and each invokes His aid against the other. It may seem strange that any men should dare ask a just God's assistance in wringing their bread from the sweat of other men's faces; but let us judge not that we be not judged. The prayers of both could not be answered; that of neither has been answered fully. The Almighty has His own purposes. "Woe unto the world because of offences! for it must needs be that offences come; but woe to that man by whom the offence cometh!" If we shall suppose that American Slavery is one of those offences which, in the providence of God, must needs come, but which, having continued through His appointed time, He now wills to remove, and that He gives to both North and South, this terrible war, as the woe due to those by whom the offence came, shall we discern therein any departure from those divine attributes which the believers in a Living God always ascribe to Him? Fondly do we hope—fervently do we pray—that this mighty scourge of war may speedily pass away. Yet, if God wills that it continue, until all the wealth piled by the bond-man's two hundred and fifty years of unrequited toil shall be sunk, and until every drop of blood drawn with the lash, shall be paid by another drawn with the sword, as was said three thousand years ago, so still it must be said "the judgments of the Lord, are true and righteous altogether."

With malice towards none; with charity for all; with firmness in the right, as God gives us to see the right, let us strive on to finish the work we are in; to bind up the nation's wounds; to care for him who shall have borne the battle, and for his widow, and his orphan —to do all which may achieve and cherish a just, and a lasting peace, among ourselves, and with all nations.

*   *   *

As Lincoln was inaugurated for his second term, the war was nearing an end. Lee's army would be surrendered in scarcely more than a month and the war would be over. It is true that the duration of the war could not be foreseen. Hope was gone for the South, but the South had fought on even without hope, and on February 9 Jefferson Davis had belatedly unloosed the best weapon of the Confederacy by appointing Lee commander in chief of all the Southern armies. But even Lee could only delay the end, not change the result. As Lincoln spoke, the outcome was not in doubt. Sherman had not only marched through Georgia to reach the sea at Savannah the previous Christmas but, despite widespread belief that it was impossible, he had successfully marched inland again into the heart of the Carolinas and the Confederacy. Less than two weeks before, on Washington's birthday, the now-completed dome of the capitol had been illuminated in celebration of Sherman's conquest of Columbia and the fall of Charleston and Wilmington. Lee and the Army of Northern Virginia were now encamped near Richmond, menaced by Grant.

The fratricidal war had torn at the land for all of Lincoln's first term, but now it would soon be over, and the armies would lay down their arms. Could the two become one again? At this moment, with the past not finished and the future but hope and foreboding, Lincoln delivered his inaugural address, by tradition the most solemn and authoritative speech of a President. The subject of Lincoln's Second Inaugural is the ground on which the two sections might be rejoined; its intent is to point away from war towards reunion. The judgment of his country has been that it was a speech in no way inferior to the tradition begun by Washington, either for the occasion on which it was delivered or for the question which it raises. It has elicited the admiration and elevated the spirit of Americans. And yet, as we have already noted, it has also puzzled them. The explicit theological language of the address is hard to assess. Let us examine the speech more closely.

Studied Simplicity

Lincoln's Second Inaugural consists of four paragraphs. The first explains why an extended address is not occasioned; the last is an exhortation to the task ahead. The middle paragraphs, the second and third, examine the war and its cause in terms of the intentions and prayers of men, and the purposes of God.

As with many of Lincoln's speeches, the simplicity of the first paragraph is almost naive. It gives three reasons why an extended address, appropriate for the First Inaugural, is inappropriate for the Second. Public declarations during the previous four years mean that little new remains to be presented; the progress of the army, upon which all else depends, is as well known to the public as to Lincoln himself; and, although he has high hopes, he will not indulge in predictions of the future. What Lincoln says in this paragraph is simple and obvious, when stated. It is one of the characteristics of Lincoln's speeches that he does not forget the obvious in pursuing the less obvious. Some have interpreted this as a lack of sophistication. Indeed, as Hofstadter has noted, Lincoln's "simplicity was very real. He called his wife 'mother,' received distinguished guests in shirtsleeves, and once during his presidency hailed a soldier out of the ranks with the cry: 'Bub! Bub!'" But Hofstadter correctly adds, ". . . he was also a complex man, easily complex enough to know the value of his own simplicity."[1]

The address will be misinterpreted if the paragraph is seen as merely an extraneous, slightly amusing, apology for unusual brevity. Lincoln's obvious points color the meaning of the less obvious. The audience knows what Lincoln knows concerning the plans, progress, and future of the war. The implication is that one should utilize a speech to say something which the listeners do not already know; if Lincoln follows his own advice, he should teach us something new.

The reasons given by Lincoln in themselves embody the structure and help to determine the meaning of the remainder of the speech. They form a temporal progression: the first reason concerns the plans laid in the past, the second the present state of affairs, and the third what is to be expected in the future. The first reason concerns the plans or intentions about the war, the second the power to fulfill these plans, and the third the effects that will result. This temporal progression of plan, power, and result is the chief organizing principle of the speech, and is present in whole or in part both in the structure of the speech as a whole and in the structure of each of its three major parts. Thus the speech as a whole moves from the present compared with the past, to the present in the center of the speech, to the action in the future in the final paragraph. A similar progression takes place within the second and third paragraphs, and the final paragraph moves from present to future. The first paragraph presents the structure of the speech as a whole and of each of its parts and invites comparison both with the whole and with the other parts.)

This parallel is not merely formal; it moderates the meaning of the other parts of the speech. The first reason for not giving an extended address is that the people know the plans for the war just as Lincoln knows them and hence there is little new to be presented. The second reason is that the people know the progress of the army as well as Lincoln. All else depends upon this progress. If the North wins, it will be because its armies defeat the Southern armies. If these points seem trivial, it is nevertheless noteworthy that Lincoln has not forgotten them. By comparing these points to the structurally similarly placed ones in the third paragraph we can see their importance. Whatever Lincoln means in the third paragraph by viewing the war as the plan of God, he does not mean that the plans for the war are not the same as they have been or that victory does not rest with him whose army is victorious. Whatever we may find Lincoln to be saying about the will of God, that will is not a substitute for human foresight or military victory. This fact is of utmost importance and, of course, immediately distinguishes Lincoln's opinion from the common piety that expects God's providence to remedy human failure.)

The third reason for the inappropriateness of a long speech is that, although Lincoln has high hopes, he will make no predictions of the future. Though he may later speculate about the purposes of God in bringing on the war, an acknowledgement of the justice of God's purposes does not provide him with the knowledge of the outcome or the course of the war. Providence does not furnish men knowledge of the future—and so is not a substitute for their foresight—any more than it substitutes for their armies.

The first paragraph shows Lincoln's awareness of the need for human foresight and effort—a need not obviated by any actions of God. The simplicity of the paragraph is not foolish simplicity.

The Failure of Human Intentions

The heart of Lincoln's speech, the second and third paragraphs, is a compact piece of rhetoric. It is divided by the sentence: "The Almighty has His own purposes." The part prior to this sentence examines the purposes and prayers of men. It concludes that neither the intentions nor the prayers of men have been fulfilled by the course of the war. The part following the sentence examines the purposes of God and concludes that the judgment of God must be said to be just if the war is a punishment for the sin of slavery. The heart of the speech as a whole attempts to end the war in men's minds (even as it would soon be ended on the battlefield) by convincing men that the war is a completed action and that justice has been done. If men are convinced that justice has been served, men need no longer be the warriors of justice. Charity can then rule men's actions. To see the force of Lincoln's argument, we must follow the course of his gentle yet compelling persuasion with some care.

Lincoln first examines the possibility that the war can'be understood as the fulfillment of human plans. In the second paragraph Lincoln characterizes the attitudes toward war of North and South four years before, in 1860. "All dreaded it—all sought to avert it." "One of them would *make* war rather than let the nation survive; and the other would *accept* war rather than let it perish." The most immediate practical question of the war was whether the nation would survive or perish. But why did one side wish to destroy and the other to save the Union?

At the beginning of the third paragraph, Lincoln examines the cause of the war—slavery. "All knew that this interest was, somehow, the cause of the war." Neither North nor South knew precisely how slavery was the cause. The Southerners wished to "strengthen, perpetuate, and extend" it while the Northerners claimed only the right to restrict its enlargement. Again Lincoln points to a distinction between the belligerents—one wished to extend, the other claimed not the right to contract but only to restrict. Both North and South took a position with regard to the known cause of the war, but they did not clearly see the sense in which slavery was the cause of the war; they were similar in their ignorance.

Up to this point in the address, Lincoln has characterized the attitudes of men toward war, toward union, and toward slavery. The South dreaded war, desired secession, and wished to strengthen and enlarge slavery—even by war. The North dreaded war, desired union, and wished to restrict the enlargement of slavery—even if it had to accept war.

But these intentions cannot wholly explain the war. Neither side had sufficient foresight to perceive what would actually result, for neither with regard to war nor to slavery did the results conform with intentions. Neither side saw the magnitude or the duration of the war; neither anticipated "that the *cause* of the conflict might cease with, or even before, the conflict itself should cease. Each looked for a result less fundamental and astounding." Both parties intended war in a sense, since one preferred it to union, the other to disunion; but the intentions of neither side controlled the results. Men did not accurately foresee the actual alternatives facing them. How was it that the war and slavery developed contrary to all expectations? Human plans and foresight do not supply the answer, but accident and chance. The war did not develop as men intended; its cause was ended before it was ended.

Although Lincoln characterizes the attitudes of both sides towards union, he does not compare these attitudes with the result. The reason for this omission is clear: the Union is a problem that is not settled by ending the war and settling the slavery issue. Is it not possible that here too neither the intention of the North nor that of the South would be fulfilled: that the nation might remain undivided and yet not united? Union is a problem because the intentions of neither side have been fulfilled and hence the situation is different than anticipated. To fulfill the present intention of reuniting the North and the South, one must see why past intentions have failed. One must ask what, if anything, actually governed the war and the end of slavery to find the end to which they are directed. To solve the problem of union, Lincoln must find the meaning of slavery and the Civil War.

Judge Not

Lincoln next turns to a discussion of the piety and prayers of men. Why Lincoln does this, when he had found that men's intentions did not give order to the Civil War, is not immediately clear. Indeed, it seems to be irrational. Lincoln poses a question, but

seems to abandon the use of his reason to answer it. To search for
the meaning of the war in piety seems to be a surrender of human
reason to divine power. Not finding the answer to his question,
Lincoln takes refuge in mysticism. However, if it is remembered
that the problem is to find the order and meaning of the Civil War,
an explanation is forthcoming.

Men may be the cause of the war in two ways: by necessitating a
particular effect or by disposing certain events, a matter of influence
rather than command. The difference may be seen in this example.
An officer may order a soldier to do a task, thus necessitating its
doing, or a soldier may ask or beseech an officer for a favor, thus
disposing the officer to a certain decision.

Now prayer supplicates a superior and thus disposes him to a
certain action. If men had directed the war through their intentions,
they would have been a perfect cause of the war because the result
necessarily followed from their intention. If they directed the war
through their prayers, they are an imperfect cause because they
were not ordering but asking. Asking is related to commanding as
the imperfect to the perfect because it reflects only a defect of
authority or power. It does not reflect a defect of reason. Asking is
but the way an inferior gives order through a superior. Prayer does
not reflect a defect of human knowledge of the proper order, but
only a defect of power. It is thus an act of reason and not, as might
be supposed, an acknowledgment of the limitations of reason.[3]
If men could dispose events through their prayers, their prayers
would make the events intelligible.

However, the meaning is not to be found in prayer either. It is not
found in what men wished for, any more than in what they had
intended. Each side approaches God in the same way. "Both read
the same Bible, and pray to the same God; and each invokes His aid
against the other." Here, too, Lincoln sees both the similarities and
differences between the positions of the North and the South. Do
those supporting slavery have as much right to ask God's assistance
as those opposing it? Can the unjust equally with the just invoke
God? The question is answered by Lincoln with the words opening
the seventh chapter of Matthew: ". . . let us judge not that we be
not judged." We must be careful in establishing the meaning of this
injunction. The words do not answer the question as to the justice
of the South's approach to God; they merely affirm that it is not for
the North to judge. But why ought not the North judge?

Lincoln does not forbid all judgments. In the final paragraph he says that men should strive on to finish the work they are in ". . . with firmness in the right, as God gives us to see the right . . ." Furthermore, looking to other occasions, one finds Lincoln making judgments on what seems to be the same issue as that posed in the Second Inaugural. On occasion, Lincoln was perfectly willing to judge the religion of the South, not only in terms of its political effect, but in terms of its religious efficacy. Only three months before the inaugural, he wrote and signed the following account of an interview:

> On thursday (sic) of last week two ladies from Tennessee came before the President asking the release of their husbands held as prisoners of war at Johnson's Island. They were put off till friday, when they came again, and were again put off to saturday. At each of the interviews one of the ladies urged that her husband was a religious man. On saturday the President ordered the release of the prisoners, and then said to this lady "You say your husband is a religious man; tell him when you meet him, that I say I am not much of a judge of religion, but that, in my opinion, the religion that sets men to rebel and fight against their government because, as they think, that government does not sufficiently help *some* men to eat their bread on the sweat of *other* men's faces, is not the sort of religion upon which people can get to heaven!⁴

On another occasion he said that those who read the Bible to say that "In the sweat of *other men's* faces shalt thou eat bread,":

> . . . condemned and insulted God and His church, far more than did satan when he tempted the Saviour with the Kingdoms of the earth. The devil's attempt was no more false, and far less hypocritical.⁵

Both the speech itself and the examples taken from outside it should warn us that we must look to the context to see what should or should not be judged.

By using a quotation, however, Lincoln sends us to the Bible. The reason given by the Bible for the injunction against judgment is that the measure one gives will be the measure by which one is measured. It is, in other words, because of the inadequacy of one's own measure that one should not judge others. It is perfectly appropriate to judge when one's own measure is adequate. But in what respect is one's own measure inadequate in the present case? It is inadequate in measuring whether the South should dare to ask a just God for assistance, because it has been shown that the North's prayers have not been entirely successful: "The prayers of both could not be answered; that of neither has been answered fully." If God has not found the prayers of the South entirely pleasing to Him, neither does the evidence indicate that He has found the North's prayers entirely pleasing for He has not answered their prayers either. "The Almighty has His own purposes."

Lincoln implicitly suggests three possible reasons for this inadequate measure. First, it is strange for the South to ask God for assistance because the South is asking for something unjust. Since no man would dare to ask for an unjust thing from a just God, the South must be ignorant of what is just. If this is so, then the injunction to judge not that we be not judged, implying an equality between North and South, raises the possibility that the actions of the North have not proceeded entirely from justice either. The North ought not to judge because its own measure has not been wholly just.

Second is the reason suggested by the actual inadequacy of the North's plans and prayers concerning the war. One ought not to make rash judgments about uncertain things. But are the motives of the prayers of the South not one of those uncertain things, depending upon inward intentions, which the North ought not to judge?

The most important reason, however, is the third, suggested by the line, "The Almighty has his own purposes." The purposes of God are not those of men, and men have not discerned the purposes of God. Hence we ought not to judge concerning how pleased God may be with the South because his purposes are not known by us. We have no authority to judge that which is above us because we do not know it. The assertion, "judge not," must be seen in its context. Lincoln does not say that the justice of the Southern cause is equivalent to that of the North. He does, however, find an equality between the North and the South in the inadequacy of both their measures. The proof of this inadequacy is the failure of both their intentions and prayers.

This equality between the North and the South, however, is an insufficient basis for union. If men merely recognize that not everything they desire will come about, there is no reason for common action for no desire could be preferred on these grounds. If all desires are limited, the just ones of the North as well as the unjust ones of the South, there would be no more reason for uniting North and South than Mexicans and Ukranians, for there would be nothing in particular that Americans share. Such a union would be arbitrary or no union at all)

Men are neither the masters of history nor its disposers through prayer. Human foresight was mistaken and human piety did not receive what it prayed for. A third possibility remains—that men are not the source of the meaning of the war. "The Almighty has His own purposes." The speech is in the form of a search for the meaning of the war, examining the possibilities in order from more apparent to less. The remainder of the central part of the speech examines God's purposes and justice. We will first summarize this part of the speech, then show the meaning it gives to the Civil War and its contribution to solving the problem of union)

The Purpose of God

The Almighty's purposes are expressed in the words of Matthew 18:7: "Woe unto the world because of offences! for it must needs be that offences come; but woe to that man by whom the offence cometh!" Lincoln applies this quotation to the present circumstances by asking a question and then answering it. The question is an unexpected one. It is neither, "What are the purposes of God in the present situation?" nor "What is the relationship between God's purposes and men's in the present situation?" but, "Assuming God's purposes, what are we to say about His qualities?":

> If we shall suppose that American Slavery is one of those offences which, in the providence of God, must needs come, but which, having continued through His appointed time, He now wills to remove, and that He gives to both North and South, this terrible war, as the woe due to those by whom the offence came, shall we discern therein any departure from those divine attributes which the believers in a living God always ascribe to Him?

Lincoln does not claim to know what the purposes of God are, but only supposes them. Suppose they are such, what then can we say about God?)

He next explains what the answer to this hypothetical question is not. The answer has nothing to do with whether one likes the war, or whether the war is terrible. Those things are clear: "Fondly do we hope—fervently do we pray—that this mighty scourge of war may speedily pass away."[6] To affirm the justice of God's attributes under these presumed purposes is not, according to Lincoln, to reduce or eliminate the horror of war: the war remains terrible and the people continue to hope and pray that it will speedily pass away. Yet,

> . . . if God wills that it continue, until all the wealth piled by the bond-man's two hundred and fifty years of unrequited toil shall be sunk, and until every drop of blood drawn with the lash, shall be paid by another drawn with the sword, as was said three thousand years ago, so still it must be said "the judgments of the Lord, are true and righteous altogether."

Lincoln answers, in the words of Psalm 19:9, that the judgments of the Lord must be said to be just, not only under the supposition that the Civil War is a punishment for the sin of slavery but even should the punishment be continued until the bond-man's wealth be sunk and the lash's blood be paid for with the sword.

Thus Lincoln finds the order in God which he found wanting in human intentions and prayers. The believers in a living God have been right, the judgments of God are true and just. The war considered as a punishment of God has meaning because it is directed toward the end of God's justice.

It must be admitted that this is a strange conclusion. Lincoln claims to have found the meaning of the war in a mixture of piety and conjecture. He takes a Biblical quotation as authority, and then applies it to present circumstances. Taking his hypothetical assumptions about God's purposes as true, he then confesses that God's judgments must be said to be just. If American slavery is one of the offences which must needs come and which God now wills to remove, and if He gives the war as the woe due to those by whom the offence came, then it is established with the Psalms that God's judgments are true and just. We must try to understand Lincoln.

Lincoln's Knowledge of God's Purposes

As we have said, Lincoln does not claim to know that God causes the war. He does not assert that God was the author of the Civil

War, as a playwright is the author of a play. The only statements made about the relationship of the Civil War to God are conditional, and the only affirmation made concerns not the causes of the Civil War but the justice of God's judgment under assumed conditions. Furthermore, the hypothetical conditions under which Lincoln affirms that the judgments of God could be declared just are not restricted to the actual circumstances of the war. The judgments of God would be just even if the war continued until all the bondman's wealth should be destroyed and the blood drawn with the lash paid for with the sword, conditions which existed neither at the time of Lincoln's speech nor at the end of the war.

In seeking to understand what Lincoln does claim to know about the purposes of God, we have the testimony of Lincoln upon the precise point in the letter to Thurlow Weed written shortly after the inaugural, which we mentioned earlier. Lincoln wrote that he expected the Second Inaugural to wear as well as and perhaps better than anything he had written. However, it was not immediately popular:

> Men are not flattered by being shown that there has been a difference of purpose between the Almighty and them. To deny it, however, in this case, is to deny that there is a God governing the world. It is a truth which I thought needed to be told; and as whatever of humiliation there is in it, falls most directly on myself, I thought others might afford for me to tell it.

The truth which Lincoln said he taught is that there is a difference of purpose between the Almighty and men. The central contention of the speech, as testified by both the structure of the speech and Lincoln's explicit claim, is "The Almighty has His own purposes."

Lincoln makes no claim to know God's purposes, but claims only to see that they are different from the purposes of men. But how does he see this if he does not see God's purposes? Is it not necessary to know both things in order to compare them?

To see that the dimly seen is different than the more clearly seen, it is not necessary to know fully that which is only dimly seen. We may use Lincoln's letter to Weed to make his assertion more intelligible. In that letter he says that to deny that there is a difference of purpose between the Almighty and men "is to deny that there is a

God governing the world." To put it positively, if there is a God governing the world, his purposes cannot be the same as men's for neither men's intentions nor their prayers are the governing source of the world, as we have seen. What Lincoln perceives is a gulf between men's purposes and God's and he comes to this perception be seeing the imperfection of men's purposes. He sees God's purposes only as they become manifest through men's purposes. What thus becomes clear is not the content of His purposes, since Lincoln does not know His plan, but that those purposes differ from men's.

This central truth is placed immediately following the discussion of prayer, and reveals the importance of prayer. While prayer is rational in regard to its content, it is folly to believe that God can be given directions even through men's prayers. To ask God for something assumes that men's reasons may govern the world. But the Almighty has His own purposes. Prayer shares the limits of human reason, but does not confess them. Because Lincoln sees the limits of men's purposes and prayers, he is able to see that they are not God's.

These limits can be seen by human reason. Lincoln confesses the limits of human reason, but does not claim to know what lies beyond the limits. However, he does speculate. The assertion is a leap in the argument which has been justified only hypothetically. Men's purposes are not God's, if there is a God. This formulation reveals the kinship of the Second Inaugural to that skepticism for which Lincoln was noted among his friends.[8] He finds limits to human intentions and achievements and does not claim to know God's purposes. The faith which regards providence as essentially unknowable and the skepticism of all providence agree that the pattern of future events cannot be known and hence that men's capacity to manage the future is limited.[9] Man's capacity to do justice is limited.

Lincoln's skepticism does not claim to know history or master nature. In a perceptive essay, Edmund Wilson attempts to identify Lincoln's discussion of providence with the latter view and attributes to him a Marxist conception of history—that of "a power which somehow takes possession of men and works out its intentions through them. . . . a kind of superhuman force that vindicates and overrides and that manipulates mankind as its instruments."[10] The difficulty in making this identification is well illustrated by the quotation Wilson brings forward to prove it. In one of the debates with Douglas, Lincoln said:

> Accustomed to trample on the rights of others, you have lost the genius of your own independence, and become the fit subjects of the first cunning tyrant who rises among you. And let me tell you that all these things are prepared for you with the logic of history, if the elections shall promise that the next Dred Scott decision and all future decisions will be quietly acquiesced in by the people.[11]

A strange sort of superhuman historical force that depends on the results of an election whose outcome Lincoln clearly regards as within human choice! Rather, as the Second Inaugural shows, Lincoln does not claim to know anything about the workings of history except that it has not been governed by men's intentions and prayers. Nor is Lincoln skeptical of the possibility of ethical judgments. He does not deny, indeed he affirms, that the South is the aggressor, the North the agressed upon, and that slavery is unjust.

It is in the light of the gulf between the purposes of men and those of God that the remainder of the paragraph is illuminated. "Woe unto the world because of offences! for it must needs be that offences come; but woe unto him by whom the offence cometh!" How can men be justly given woe for offences which "must needs" come? Strange as it seems, this quotation at least expresses the dilemma of Lincoln if he is to remain true to the problem he faces. On the one hand, the Civil War is terrible, bringing suffering and misery. If the Civil War is to have meaning, it must both be part of an order and an offence, a disorder—a seeming impossibility. The resolution of this dilemma comes when the quotation is seen within the context of the assertion that "The Almighty has His own purposes."

The quotation is applied by designating slavery as the offence and war as the woe. Lincoln says: "If we shall suppose that American slavery is one of those offences which, in the providence of God, must needs come, but which, having continued through His appointed time, He now wills to remove. . . ." The key to understanding this supposition is the words, "in the providence of God." What does it mean to assert that slavery is one of those offences, which, in the providence of God, must needs come?

The providence of God stands opposed to the providence of men. Lincoln adds "in the providence of God" as an explanatory phrase in his repetition of the Biblical quotation, as if to emphasize that slavery was not necessary in the providence of men. He goes on to say that the offence (slavery) came, not by God, but by the actions of both North and South.

The providence of God, as does all providence, directs to an end. Hence the offence must be necessary in relation to that end, if it "must needs come" in the providence of God. Now we must remember that the purposes of God are not those of men, which means that the end to which God directs is not the same as the end to which man directs. God is not simply "Nature's God" of the Declaration of Independence, but a mysterious God whose purposes are other than those of man by nature. Since the ends differ, the governing differs. Hence it is possible for something to be necessary in the providence of God without being necessary in the providence of man. Something may be accidental to man's government yet necessary to God's.

What, then, does Lincoln claim to know about the war? Lincoln affirms that it must be said that "the judgments of the Lord are true and righteous altogether" even if:

> God wills that it [the war] continue, until all the wealth piled by the bond-man's two hundred and fifty years of unrequited toil shall be sunk, and until every drop of blood drawn with the lash, shall be paid by another drawn with the sword. . . .

It is not the war, considered as a human action, but punishment for the sin of slavery which Lincoln affirms to be just. Lincoln's assertion is in the form: if the war were a punishment, God's judgment would be just. But it is not from a human viewpoint that the Civil War can be seen as a punishment for slavery. Only if we suppose it to be the will of God can it be seen as punishment.

To say that the Civil War is a just punishment is not to consider it to be a just action on the part of the South. Here one must distinguish between end and means. Regarded as an end to which other things are referred, the war is not necessarily just, and indeed Lincoln does not believe it to be so. It is a terrible war. "Fondly do we hope—fervently do we pray—that this mighty scourge of war shall pass away." But that the war, considered as an end of man's actions, is unjust does not mean that the war, considered as a means effecting God's purposes, is not just. Thus if one boy hits another, an adult may be able to use the event to try to teach the one hit the virtue of enduring pain. This beneficent teaching does not mean that it was just for one boy to hit the other, even though the lesson could not have been taught otherwise, and even though the parent may have let his child get into the situation where he was liable to be hit.

Regarded as a divine event the Civil War is given the meaning of divine punishment for the sin of slavery, but this does not give the war the status of a suitable end of men's actions. From the view of man, the Civil War has no meaning because it was caused by injustice and accident.

War and Slavery

It is not because of the horror of the Civil War that Lincoln regards the war as the punishment of God. It is rather because he sees the injustice of slavery that he can perceive that the punishment would be just if the Civil War were punishment; if the war is a punishment of God, it is just. The misinterpretation of Lincoln's words shifts attention away from the sin of slavery to the horror of the war. If the war is so horrible, may it not be the punishment of God for some sin?

Lincoln actually finds meaning in the war only by diverting his glance from the war and fixing it on slavery. The injustice of slavery means that punishment is deserved. Lincoln's position on the sin of slavery and the justice of punishment would remain whether there was a war or not. However, horror of war was easier for most men to see than was the sin of slavery (as it is easier to see one's own suffering than injustice to another). Lincoln uses the more easily known truth, the horror of war, to reveal the less obvious but more decisive truth, the sin of slavery. To believe that God sent the war as punishment causes one to believe that slavery is unjust. Lincoln thus attempts to share something of the more difficult truth by means of the more easily understood truth. In the process he does not hide the truth from those who seek it but reveals as much of it as possible to those who do not.

In revealing the sin of slavery through the horror of war, Lincoln is trying to persuade his audience, not by using reason alone, but by using rhetoric. Nevertheless Lincoln's speech must be distinguished from the imposition of propaganda for two reasons. First, he reveals his true interpretation of the war to those who seek it. He teaches the truth, merely allowing a reader who is not careful to reach another conclusion. Second, the interpretation which Lincoln allows is directed towards conveying the crucial truth — that slavery is unjust. He seeks to convey a correct moral opinion by means of people's feelings of pleasure and pain. While Lincoln is imposing an interpretation in a sense, it is an interpretation which brings men closer to, not further, from the truth as he sees it. Lincoln seeks to create a public opinion that is neither fully rational nor merely imposed belief, but partly rational and partly *self*-imposed belief.

Lincoln seeks to use belief to make men aware of the limits of their reason. Men, as their prayers reveal, are not aware of the limits of their own governing, and hence are not perfectly rational animals. Pleasure and pain must come to the support of reason. Just as one seeks to bring a criminal to justice by means of punishment, so the people can be brought to justice only be means of punishment. Punishment is a way of revealing to those who do not obey the laws by their own wills. Punishment equalizes excesses.

This is so, of course, whether or not the criminal considers his punishment just. However, if he does consider it just he has been restored to justice in a fuller sense. He shares in the just order he acknowledges. It is not merely imposed upon him. In a democracy the people are not criminals, but free men who cannot be ruled by punishment they consider unjust; they must acknowledge the justice of their punishment. They must share in the order of justice as does the reformed criminal, not merely as does he who has "done his time." Punishment is necessary in order to restore excess to equality; but it must be punishment that the people admit to be just punishment.

Hence Lincoln does not argue that the Civil War is a punishment, but seeks to gain men's assent to the proposition. Both the question he asks and the answer he gives are concerned not with God's purposes, but with men's perception and action. He asks, "shall we discern. . . ?"; he replies, "so still it must be said . . ." The question asks, "What do we see?"; but Lincoln responds as if the question had been, "What must we say?" Lincoln must make men aware that their purposes are not God's, but they do not see this by their reason. Lincoln attempts to point it out to them by using the more easily perceived truth, the horror of war, to reveal the harder truth, the sin of slavery and hence the limits of their intentions. To do this, it must be supposed that God is governing the world and that he gives the war as punishment. This providence cannot be shown by reason. One can only testify to its truth. The response to the question must be that "it must be *said*" that the judgments of the Lord are true and righteous. The things of reason may be shown; those of faith can only be confessed.)

By acknowledging the sin of slavery and the justice of God one has made the most crucial step in solving the problem of union, for the injustice which led to the war has been recognized as injustice.

With Malice Towards None

Lincoln's practical aim in the Second Inaugural is to instill a spirit in the people which would lead them to support his policies for reunion. Reunion could not be built upon the hatreds of the war, nor by giving up justice. One had to combine justice with charity. Lincoln had to form the people to justice and charity if his policies were to be successful)

Lincoln could do this only insofar as he succeeded in teaching an opinion. Men must acknowledge that the war is a just punishment of God for the sin of slavery. Their suffering would then reveal that the sin of slavery, the cause of the war, was due to the North as well as the South. While the injustice of the South — the desire to extend slavery — was, in a sense, the cause of the war; in another sense, North and South were equals. They were equal in the eyes of God, *i.e.*, both sinners through the injustice of slavery. It was possible to be charitable to the South because one was not thereby denying justice, but acknowledging the justice of God's punishment. Human charity requires divine vengeance. Lincoln's counsel of charity is not a sentimental sympathy for the South that ignores the stern dictates of justice. In punishment and confession North and South become equal and are restored to justice. Lincoln uses the war to reveal that men are equally under God's judgment. He reveals that they had been living under judgment all along, even before the war, although they knew it not.)

Lincoln thus leads men to acknowledge limits to their government. Their actions must be bounded by an order they did not create. Lincoln teaches the people to be reasonable or moderate by teaching than an exact justice is to be left to God alone. It can be left to Him alone because the war demonstrates the justice of His providence. That passsion for a cold or inhuman justice that would demand an eye for an eye is moderated by a human charity that rests upon divine retribution.)

(In the Second Inaugural Lincoln teaches that the people must be formed, not only informed, because their passions can only be controlled by counter-passions, not by a mere statement of the truth. It is necessary for the passions to be controlled because even the government of the people is not unlimited. But the people must impose the limits on themselves if such a government is to be ultimately successful. Lincoln found the possibility of such self-limitation in belief in a God whose purposes were not those of men, whose purposes could not be known, but could nevertheless be recognized to be just. Lincoln saw in religion not the threat to political moderation alleged by Masters, but the inner source of moderation in a self-governing people when that religion was properly taught by men such as himself. Today we find ourselves in different circumstances than those Lincoln faced on that March day in 1864, perhaps more so with regard to the resources we have that a statesman can utilize to teach moderation than in the reasons why that moderation is still necessary. But Lincoln shows us that our vexing problems cannot be solved without reflecting on the very foundations of our political order—without reflecting on the need for limitations in the people themselves and the challenge that need presents to our faith in a moderate politics without religion)

(But if we compare the Second Inaugural with the Gettysburg Address, we are faced with another problem. The universal purposes to which Lincoln dedicated the nation anew in the earlier address are now gone from view. There the nation was dedicated to the proposition that all men are created equal and upon its fate rested the great question of whether government of, by and for the people would perish from the earth. But if men do not govern the course of history, if the Almighty has His own purposes, then human action cannot prove or disprove a proposition. Men may fail to prove it because of some accident. One cannot know the experience of one nation to be decisive because God's purposes are not men's. The Gettysburg Address left men with a task decisive for all mankind, Americans and nonAmericans, living and dead. The Second Inaugural leaves men to:

> strive on to finish the work we are in; to bind up the nation's wounds; to care for him who shall have borne the battle, and for his widow, and his orphan—to do all which may achieve and cherish a just, and a lasting peace, among ourselves, and with all nations.

Is it possible that Lincoln's two most famous speeches stand in fundamental contradiction to each other, the one infusing the nation with a universal task, the other asserting that the actions of one nation cannot be decisive because the Almighty has His own purposes?)

VI.

CONCLUSION:
TRANSCENDING POLITICS

Both the Gettysburg Address and the Second Inaugural end with counsel for future action. The first calls the people to renewed dedication to the cause of the war; the second to achieve a just and lasting peace. It is not surprising that they end differently, for the one was written in the midst of war and the other at its end. But there is a difference between the two speeches that is surprising and even disconcerting.

Both speeches base their recommendations on an interpretation of the same event, the Civil War. But the interpretations given by the two addresses seem to be in fundamental contradiction. Not only the actions recommended but the understanding that informs these recommendations seems to differ. Different actions would have to be recommended by a wise statesman in the different circumstances of the two speeches, but could the fundamental understanding of the war change?

The Gettysburg Address, as we have seen, endows the actions of the living with encompassing significance. The purposes of the war were set by our fathers when they brought forth the new nation. The dead gave their lives that this nation might live. Our fathers' work and the sacrifice of the soldiers at Gettysburg will be in vain unless the living take renewed dedication to their cause. The responsibility of the living extends to the past as well as the future, but the test of this responsibility does not merely extend backward and forward. The war not only tests whether *this* nation can long endure, but whether *any* nation so conceived and dedicated can long endure. We are responsible to the whole world, not merely to ourselves.

The great responsibility which the Gettysburg Address lays upon men results from the crucial significance of the present action, which is the decisive testing of a theoretical argument. Lincoln forms the war into a test or proof of whether a nation dedicated to the proposition that all men are created equal can long endure. Because this proposition is the fundamental principle of the country and the foundation of the morality of all people, the country and one's own moral being depend upon the perpetuation of this principle. The principle is a proposition which must be proved through action; the war will show whether it is possible to found a country on this principle and hence whether it is possible to prove the proposition true. The war is not simply an illustration of certain theoretical principles, or a test of those principles in a certain set of circumstances, but *the* decisive test. Salvation can be achieved only through renewed dedication to the cause for which the dead gave their last full measure of devotion.

Although Lincoln does not claim to know the results of the war in the Gettysburg Address, he does claim to know the significance of the alternative outcomes. The war will test whether "that nation or any nation so conceived and so dedicated can long endure." The historical significance of human actions are known because all depends on those actions: victory or defeat is decisive. In defeat the sacrifice of the dead will be in vain.

It is precisely this encompassing of life and death within the perspective of national purposes and actions that the Second Inaugural appears to deny. While the Gettysburg Address endows actions with encompassing significance in history, the Second Inaugural seems to draw limits to their significance. The action recommended seems tame in comparison with the decisive actions required at Gettysburg:

> . . . let us strive on to finish the work we are in; to bind up the nation's wounds; to care for him who shall have borne the battle, and for his widow, and his orphan — to do all which may achieve and cherish a just, and a lasting peace, among ourselves, and with all nations.

The actions counseled are practical and limited; they are not part of a theoretical enterprise. The universal principles which men's actions were to demonstrate have disappeared.

Moreover, human actions seem not to be supreme. The speech attempts to show that human purposes have not been fulfilled and that they have led to unexpected results—they have not governed events. There can be no unqualified meaning given to human actions by looking at their historical results because the unexpected may happen. The Gettysburg Address seems to deny chance or God's providence. The Second Inaugural asserts that human purposes and actions are not theoretically decisive, only illustrative: one cannot know the meaning of the Civil War; one can only say that if God intended it as a punishment, God is just.

The Second Inaugural and the Gettysburg Address thus present contradictory understandings of the same phenomenon, the Civil War. In the Gettysburg Address men's actions are theoretically and historically decisive; in the Second Inaugural human purposes and actions are neither theoretically nor historically decisive. In the Gettysburg Address, the war is a decisive test of a universal principle; in the Second Inaugural the principles governing the war are not known because the "Almighty has His own purposes."

Sacred Principles and Self-Determination

Richard Hofstadter has argued that the Civil War can not be seen as a defense of the "sacred principles of popular rule," as Lincoln thought. Rather, "What the North was waging, of course, was a war to save the Union by denying self-determination to the majority of Southern whites."[1] To weigh this opinion, we must consider Lincoln's peculiar position.

Lincoln was elected President of the United States, yet he became leader of one part of the United States in a war against the other part. While he claimed to be President of all, this claim was resisted by the South who considered itself to have the Constitutional right to withdraw from the Union, and had a sufficiently powerful army to resist Lincoln's claim for the length of his tenure in office. In terms of control of territory and allegiance of the people, Lincoln was President of only a part of the United States.

Lincoln always argued that the South had no legal right to secede. He and the North were obedient to the country's laws; the South was disobedient through rebellion. But we are not here concerned with Lincoln's constitutional arguments, important as they are in understanding his actions. Rather we are concerned with the relationship between the country and the "sacred principles of popular rule." This relationship is prior to Lincoln's constitutional arguments.

In principle, Lincoln contended that to lead the North and to lead the United States were one and the same. This contention is suggested by the Gettysburg Address when it maintains that the principles for which the North was waging the war were the principles of "our fathers" who had brought forth the Union. They were the principles of the fathers of the South as well as the North. Because the nation dedicated to these principles would be lost if they were lost, those who rebelled against them could only be rebelling against the whole nation. That it was merely the North which now upheld the principles did not prove that they were merely the principles of a part, but rather that only a part was loyal to the principles of the whole. Those loyal to the North were loyal to the part representing the whole.

Victory in the war was to be a victory for these principles. Because Lincoln sought to restore the principles of our fathers through the war, there was no conflict between his role as Northern war leader and as President of the United States. To impose the principles of the North upon the South was not to impose partisan principles, but was to recall the South to its own principles.

But the fact that the force and loyalties of the South did not agree to this interpretation created a problem. The issue is complicated by the very principles of the North. The North not only professed to believe that all men are created equal but also professed, as a conclusion from this principle, that governments derive their just powers from the consent of the governed. As Lincoln bluntly put it, "No man is good enough to govern another man, without that man's consent."[2] One could argue that the South had given its consent at the time of original Union and that it could not now be withdrawn. This is indeed the burden of much of Lincoln's constitutional argument. But neither the Declaration nor Lincoln denies the extra-legal right of the people to withdraw their consent in certain circumstances. The Declaration acknowledges this right "whenever any Form of Government becomes destructive of these ends [securing men's rights and basing government on consent]." The Declaration does not acknowledge a right to rebel in those who deny its principles, but it does to those who affirm them in certain circumstances.

As we have seen, the Declaration assumes that the principles that are true in themselves also will become true for us. If they do not, however, what happens to this right of rebellion? There are then two necessary criteria for a government which may legitimately claim men's loyalties: it must secure their rights and it must gain their consent. But these principles do not go hand in hand: one may consent to a government that does not secure men's rights, or one may refuse to consent to a government that does. In the case of the South, its refusal to consent to the North entails the result that the powers of the North are not justly exercised over it. To be sure, the South does not secure men's rights, but the South's injustice is not a sufficient reason for the North to exercise her power against the South's wishes. One might argue that the principle that all men are created equal takes precedence over consent because the latter is but a deduction from the former. This is true, but irrelevent, for the Declaration argues that both principles are necessary in order to have just government.

The nation after the victory of the North would have to be governed by a part, because the victory of the North was not an immediate defeat of the principles of the South in the breasts of Southerners. They bowed to superior force, not to persuasion, and they were not soon to consider that force equivalent to persuasion. How could Lincoln, according to the triumphant principles, represent the whole if the South did not consent to the principles that the war had rendered triumphant? There seems to be justice in Hofstadter's contention that the war was a war of self-determination. The very victory of the North seemed to present the North with a situation in which it had to betray its own principles.

Equality and Consent

As we have seen, Lincoln changed the principles of the Founders in significant ways at Gettysburg. In changing the principle of equality from an axiom to a proposition, making it the end as well as the beginning of the country, he thereby also made consent the goal of the country. It is not sufficient to consent to any form of government, but government must be by continual consent—it must be government not only of the people, but by the people.

Now the Second Inaugural clarifies the criterion of consent by clarifying the meaning of equality. The problem of the speech, as we have noted, is to find the bases upon which the two sections could reunite. The difficulty is that the North and South must be both morally equal and morally unequal. The North and the South must be morally unequal if the war is a just war; but if the South is unjust, how can the North reunite with it without betraying its own justice? The solution of the Second Inaugural is that both North and South have been unjust in that the offence of slavery had come by them both. This did not make the two sides equally unjust for the war came by the injustices of the South. Lincoln believes at the time of the Second Inaugural that the North was waging a just war. Nevertheless both sides are unjust in the eyes of God.

Human imperfection, however, is not the ground on which the two sections may reunite, because imperfections differ and conflict. Besides, if such a union could be established, it would be a union on the ground of injustice. Instead, the ground must be a common acknowledgment of injustice. In acknowledging injustice one also acknowledges the justice by which one sees one's own acts as unjust. The country can reunite on this common ground of justice.

In order, however, to achieve a common acknowledgment of injustice, it is necessary for the people to undergo war as a punishment of God. Men have not freely consented to the fundamental moral principle; they must be brought under it by means of punishment and a punishment acknowledged as such. Only in this way are they brought back to justice. The equality of men is found when they stand equally under the judgment of God. Each is equally remote from the purposes of God; each equally acknowledges God's justice. Lincoln must teach the people that, as a people, they are under judgment.

Men are created equal in this sense whether they acknowledge it or not; however, their actual consent is just only when they actually acknowledge this equality. Only then do they acknowledge the common ground of justice, and only then are they equal. If one sees justice from a merely human point of view, one will not see men's moral equality but their moral inequality: the North is just; the South unjust. Men are morally equal in that they all come under the same judgment; all are responsible, all sinners, all capable of repentence—all capable of being brought to consent to the equality of men. One must transcend the human point of view to preserve both of the principles of the Declaration as reinterpreted by Lincoln. In so doing one does not abolish moral differences—we must have "firmness in the right as God gives us to see the right"—but finds the grounds on which moral unequals may unite without confirming injustice.)

The Gettysburg Address and the Second Inaugural

The Gettysburg Address is not so much rejected as it is transcended by the Second Inaugural. It is transcended by transcending the nation which the Gettysburg Address has been held to express so supremely. This transcendence is made very explicit. The Gettysburg Address begins with the words, "Fourscore and seven years ago," firmly establishing the horizon of the speech. Its horizon is the nation. Popular opinion has considered the address the supreme expression of American democracy; it was the nation speaking. We have seen that there is a problem with the popular opinion: Lincoln was not merely expressing what had been, but was actually reforming or recreating the nation in giving the speech. As Edmund Wilson well says:

> When we put ourselves back into the period, we realize that it was not at all inevitable to think of it as Lincoln thought, and we come to see that Lincoln's conception of the course and the meaning of the Civil War was indeed an interpretation that he partly took over from others but that he partly made others accept, and in the teeth of a good deal of resistance on the part of the North itself.[3]

But it remains true that Lincoln spoke from the viewpoint of the nation—with the qualification that it was the viewpoint of the nation he was helping create.)

The Second Inaugural, however, does not speak from the viewpoint of the nation. "As was said three thousand years ago, so still it must be said, the judgments of the Lord are true and righteous altogether."[4] It ties the present back, not to our fathers, but to those who have acknowledged the justice of God at whatever time and place, and specifically to ancient Israel. The Second Inaugural speaks standing under God's judgment.

The question asked by the Gettysburg Address is, "How can such a nation long endure?"—not whether it is true that all men are created equal. The Second Inaugural raises this more fundamental issue, "Where is equality to be found?" The same problem may appear differently within the two horizons. On the nation's part, man's responsibility is for the living and the dead, for our fathers and for the soldiers on the battlefield, and for the principles upon which the nation is founded; from the viewpoint of judgment, man's responsibility is to God for his injustices.

These perspectives do not abolish each other; neither expresses the whole truth: they are both addressed to the nation. If we do not notice their different perspectives, we would conclude that they are contradictory. But to speak to the nation means to use rhetoric. It is not possible to unite the perspectives or to find a unifying perspective because of the need for rhetoric. The perspective of the nation is necessary because it both reveals and hides: it reveals the fundamental principle of popular morality which is not seen without being embodied in a nation; it hides that which could only be misinterpreted, the inequality of the "family of the lion, or the tribe of the eagle."

Lincoln teaches that it is also necessary for the citizens of democracy to have a perspective transcending the nation. Only by seeing themselves as standing under the judgment of God will the intoxication of their own sovereignty be sobered by awareness of human limits. Only then may the principles of democracy result in justice instead of injustice.

According to Lincoln in the Lyceum Speech a democractic people is either too complacent or too aroused: it either denies human responsibility by trusting the inevitable course of events, or it denies human limitations by trusting to the experiments of man. The principles of the Founders helped to create and exacerbate these tendencies by too great a reliance on the temporary spirit of the Revolution and by praise of novelty. The result was moral indifference or a morality without prudence and compassion. Reason alone could not bring about reform of the Founders' work, but men's passions had to be brought to the aid of reason. Yet to do this by dangling before men's eyes the image of a perfected society, freed of all human weakness as well as all human evil, is to neglect the permanence of the passions and the roots of popular morality in public opinion. The essential support of the Union to the moral well-being of the citizens was thus overlooked. The habits and prudence that were necessary to preserve such a society were in turn neglected.

Lincoln's solution to this problem in the Gettysburg Address and the Second Inaugural is a political religion that teaches responsibility while allowing prudence and sets limits that allow justice while teaching compassion. The contrasting tendencies of democracy must be brought to moderation by a political religion with a dual viewpoint; one that of the nation, the other transcending it. The first would arouse men to their duties and to the nobility of their task; the second would teach them the limits of that task and the humility from which compassion might spring.

In order to do this, it was insufficient for Lincoln merely to preach religion. He had to reinterpret the viewpoint of the nation such that it would be open to the higher viewpoint. The principles of the Declaration that claimed to be complete and self-evident had to be transformed so that men would be open to higher principle, so that they would see the limits of political action as well as be aroused to the possibilities politics provides. The principle of the Declaration had to be interpreted as a democratic principle, and men brought to democratic principles by seeing themselves under judgment. Only that judgment for democractic man is not the judgment of the next world, but the overwhelmingly present one found in the war.

The two viewpoints of Lincoln's speeches stand in tension in American political religion, but that tension is not resolvable unless reason were to replace the need for political religion, or democratic principles found inferior — the very things Lincoln denies. One needs both, perhaps one more at some times than at others. The political religion can ultimately be held in proper tension only by a statesman, a man such as Lincoln.

Men must participate in God's order by acknowledging the justice of God. But they cannot transcend the nation in this sense unassisted. They need someone who will point out to them what God's judgment is. Because they are formed by the nation, they will think that God's judgment is the same as the nation's judgment, or they will substitute their private judgment for the nation's judgment, thus undermining the principles of their own better nature. They do not see by themselves that "the Almighty has His own purposes." The need of democratic citizens to transcend the nation can be fulfilled only if they have a guide who stands between God and man.

Lincoln's Moderation

Lincoln, like the temperance movement, seems to use religious passions for a secular purpose. Yet Lincoln's "political religion" has a moderation the temperance movement lacked. It is not oriented towards the future. It provides no assurance concerning one's destiny. One cannot earn salvation by participating in its cause. Since it does not claim to know what is going to happen in the future, it cannot justify present actions in terms of the future. If men's actions are not justified by reference to the future state of perfection, then reformers may escape the indifference to prudence which such an orientation implies. To the old reformers, it was no argument that their methods failed to induce reform; their failure was due to the corruption of the drunkards. Not their methods, but the drunkards were to blame. Their methods were to be judged not by their effectiveness, but by the standards of the pure state of perfection. Lincoln's rhetoric implies no such indifference to success; hence he may recognize weakness and form a moderation or tolerance that takes account of weakness. To the old reformers, who believed that perfection is possible, weakness is the same as evil. Lincoln's political religion, on the other hand, is formed from awareness of human weakness and from knowledge that men are not perfectly rational.

Lincoln's view also differs from such ideology in requiring great men and great deeds. It does not present a way of acting that is universally good; it appeals to the sacrifices and deeds of the Founders, not simply to their doctrines. It requires a man who can interpret the Founders' advice in the light of their deeds for the present time. Political religion is made just in new circumstances by being formed in the hands of a statesman. He can see what should be done and what can be done in the present time. An ideology such as the temperance one, on the other hand, presents an unchangeable standard, appropriate to the state of perfection. This standard is to be imitated now because it is attainable now. Great men and great deeds are not needed because everything necessary is known. To be sure, talented men may be able to contribute more to the temperance cause; but temperance needs no one who stands above the temperance cause and who transcends the ideology. Political religion properly understood, far from banishing prudence, requires it; the temperance ideology, far from allowing prudence, condemns it as unjust compromise with evil.

But one must also consider the difficulty of what Lincoln proposes. In rejecting all aristocratic pretentions, Lincoln enshrines the
continuing consent of the people. The people, freed of their com-
petitors, are granted a nobility certainly not granted them by the
Federalist or even Jefferson. To be sure they are to be chastised and
rendered noble by the apparent judgments of God, but is it so
surprising that the statesmen who would make those judgments
apparent have been so infrequent? Without the Second Inaugural
does the Gettysburg Address not assume a rigidity it did not have in
Lincoln's own thought?

NOTES

Preface

1. Woodrow Wilson, *Congressional Government* (New York: Meridian Books, 1956), pp. 27-28.

2. For a challenging discussion of the degree to which Wilson was responsible for this change, see Paul Eidelberg, *A Discourse on Statesmanship* (Urbana, Chicago, London: University of Illinois Press, 1974), chaps. 8-9.

3. See Harvey C. Mansfield, Jr., *Statesmanship and Party Government* (Chicago, London: University of Chicago Press, 1965), p. 17.

4. The great difference between these two groups, which should not be minimized, is that the political scientists leave open the possibility that the greatest statesmen of the past had an understanding that might still guide us today, while the historians tend to believe that the statesmen's thought, while crucial to understanding them, is irretrievably bound to their particular circumstances. Compare, for example, the introduction to Morton J. Frisch and Richard G. Stevens, eds., *American Political Thought* (New York: Scribners, 1971), with the preface to Gordon S. Wood, *The Creation of the American Republic 1776-1787* (Chapel Hill: University of North Carolina Press, 1969).

Chapter I

1. Mark De Wolfe Howe has stressed this dual concern of the Constitution in *The Garden and the Wilderness* (Chicago, London: University of Chicago Press, 1965).

2. From *A Letter Concerning Toleration*, in John Locke, *Treatise of Civil Government and A Letter Concerning Toleration*, ed. Charles L. Sherman (New York: Appleton-Century, 1937), p. 171.

3. See Robert N. Bellah, "Civil Religion in America," *Daedalus* (Winter, 1967): 1-21.

4. For a good, brief discussion of Jefferson's religion, see Harvey C. Mansfield, Jr., "Thomas Jefferson," in Frisch and Stevens, eds., *American Political Thought*, pp. 36-38.

5. Thomas Jefferson, *Notes on the State of Virginia* (New York, Evanston, London: Harper & Row, 1964), p. 156.

6. *The Writings of George Washington*, ed. John C. Fitzpatrick, 39 vols. (Washington: Superintendent of Documents, 1931-44) vol. 35, p. 229.

7. *Zorach v. Clauson*, 343 U.S. 306 (1952); *Abington School District v. Schempp*, 374 U.S. 203 (1963).

8. *McCollum v. Board of Education*, 333 U.S. 203 (1948).

9. *Zorach*, p. 313.

10. *Engel v. Vitale*, 370 U.S. 434 (1962).

11. *Abington*, p. 213.

12. Ibid., p. 214.

13. Ibid., p. 222.

14. One might interpret this to indicate the Court's opinion that the two separate traditions to which it refers are both embodied in the Constitution, although it does not say this.

15. *Abington*, p. 226.

16. Ibid., p. 222.

17. Ibid., p. 313.

18. Ibid., p. 306.

19. Robert Bellah, cited above, notes that a major change occurred in what he calls "civil religion" with the Civil War and Lincoln. He compares this change with the change from the Old to the New Testament. While he does not tell us whether these changes came about through accident or design, or explain their significance, he argues that they received their finest expression in Lincoln. Bellah, p. 18.

20. Lord Charnwood, *Abraham Lincoln* (Garden City, New York: Doubleday, 1917), p. 439.

21. Abraham Lincoln, *Collected Works*, ed. Roy P. Basler, 9 vols. (New Brunswick, New Jersey: Rutgers University Press, 1953), vol. 8, p. 333.

22. Charnwood, p. 439.

23. Quoted from notes of Herndon in Richard N. Current, *The Lincoln Nobody Knows* (New York, London, Toronto: McGraw Hill, 1958), p. 52.

24. William H. Herndon, *Lincoln's Religion*, supplement to the *State Register of Springfield*, 1873, reprinted in *Lincoln's Religion*, ed. Douglas C. McMurtrie (Chicago: Black Cat, 1936), pp. 17-18.

25. Reinhold Niebuhr, "The Religion of Abraham Lincoln," in Allan Nevins, ed., *Lincoln and the Gettysburg Address* (Urbana, Illinois: University of Illinois Press, 1964), p. 72.

26. U.S. Congress, House, *Inaugural Addresses of the Presidents of the United States*, 82d Cong., 2d Sess., 1952, House Doc. 540, p. 228.

27. Ibid., pp. 1-2.

28. Current, pp. 62-64.

29. *Collected Works*, vol. 8, p. 333.

30. J.G. Randall and Richard N. Current, *Lincoln the President: Last Full Measure*, 4 vols. (New York: Eyre, 1955), vol. 4, pp. 342, 371.

31. Matthew 7:1; Matthew 18:7; Psalms 19:9.

32. Masters argues that Lincoln's hypocrisy can be seen in the speech itself, as well as by comparing the speech to his deeds. For example, consider: "With malice toward none, with charity for all, with firmness in the right as God gives us the right to see the right, . . ." Contrast the third phrase with the first two, for it reveals a "gigantic inconsistency." While counseling charity, Lincoln also says that the North is going to continue waging war for what she considers to be right. Edgar Lee Masters, *Lincoln the Man* (New York: Dodd, Mead, & Co., 1931), pp. 471-72.

33. Ibid., p. 471.

34. William H. Herndon, Jesse W. Weik, *Life of Lincoln*, ed. Paul M. Angle (New York: Fawcett, 1961), p. 40.

35. See the argument of John Stuart Mill, "Utility of Religion," in *Nature and Utility of Religion*, ed. George Nakhnikian (New York: Bobbs Merrill, 1958), pp. 45-80.

36. *Collected Works*, vol. 8, p. 356.

37. The Gettysburg Address and the Second Inaugural will lead us to other speeches of Lincoln's, above all to the Lyceum Speech and the Temperance Address. The crucial importance of these speeches for understanding Lincoln's statesmanship has been pointed out by Harry V. Jaffa in his *Crisis of the House Divided* (Garden City, New York: Doubleday, 1959). Although a few others had guessed their importance (most notably Edmund Wilson in the case of the Lyceum Speech), Jaffa was the first to see and articulate their relevance to Lincoln's fight with Douglas.

Chapter II

1. *Collected Works*, vol. 7, p. 23.

2. Ibid., vol. 1, p. 108.

3. For a detailed description and documentation of the violence, see Albert J. Beveridge, *Abraham Lincoln: 1809-1858* (Boston, New York: Houghton Mifflin, 1928), pp. 218-231.

4. The following analysis is indebted to Jaffa's *Crisis of the House Divided*.

5. Ibid., pp. 193-195.

6. Ibid.

7. See Aristotle's distinction between the ambitious and the magnanimous or great-souled man. *Nicomachean Ethics* IV, iii-iv; II, vii, 7-9.

8. Jaffa, 205-209.

9. *Collected Works*, vol. 3, p. 357.

10. Lincoln, like the classical political scientists, looks for danger primarily from the great man, not from economic forces or social classes, because he sees the higher as having greater force than the lower. Just as it was the nobility of the Founder's conception of their government that excited men's ambition, so it is the opportunity for greatness that the great man seems to offer the people that may excite them to new enterprises. The danger comes to the country from on high.

11. See Montesquieu, *The Spirit of the Laws*, trans. Thomas Nugent (New York: Hafner, 1949), vol. 1, I.4.

12. Jaffa, p. 227.

Chapter III

1. See Charnwood, p. 455.

2. Benjamin P. Thomas, *Abraham Lincoln* (New York: Knopf, 1954), p. 496. For a compact collection of the evidence in support of the opinion, see Allan Nevins, "Lincoln's Ideas of Democracy," *Lincoln: A Contemporary Portrait* (Garden City, New York: Doubleday, 1962), pp. 1-19.

3. Woodrow Wilson, "Abraham Lincoln: A Man of the People," in *Selected Literary and Political Papers and Addresses of Woodrow Wilson*, 3 vols. (New York: Grosset, 1925), vol. 1, p. 234.

4. Ibid., p. 234-35.

5. Ibid., p. 234.

6. Ibid., p. 235.

7. *Collected Works*, vol. 4, p. 270.

8. Harry V. Jaffa, *Equality and Liberty* (New York: Oxford University Press, 1965), p. 139.

9. *Collected Works*, vol. 1, pp. 178-79.

10. Jaffa, *Crisis*, p. 27.

11. *Collected Works*, vol. 4, p. 236.

12. Ibid., vol. 2, p. 532.

13. Plato, *Republic* 563b.

14. Aristotle, *Politics* 1280a23, 1325a25-30, 1329a20-22.

15. *Collected Works*, vol. 3, pp. 326-27.

16. Ibid., vol.2, p. 255.

17. Ibid., vol.3, pp. 445-46.

18. Ibid., vol.2, pp. 264-65.

19. Ibid., vol.2, pp. 222-23.

20. Ibid., vol.2, pp. 281-82.

21. Ibid., vol.2, p. 256.

22. Richard Hofstadter, *The American Political Tradition* (New York: Knopf, 1948), p. 111.

23. *Collected Works*, vol. 2, p. 406.

24. Ibid.

25. Ibid.

26. Ibid., vol.2, p. 500, inter alia.

27. Ibid., vol.2, p. 385.

28. Ibid., vol.2, p. 499.

29. Ibid., vol.2, p. 500.

30. Ibid., vol.2, p. 341.

31. Ibid., vol.4, p. 240.

32. See the report of Tolstoy's conversation with a wild Circassian tribe, whose heroes turned out to be Napoleon and Lincoln, in Carl Sandburg, *Abraham Lincoln: The War Years*, 4 vols. (New York: Harcourt, Brace & Co., 1939), vol. 4, pp. 376-77.

33. *Collected Works*, vol. 3, pp. 204-05.

34. Ibid., vol. 2, p. 500.

35. Jaffa, *Crisis*, pp. 211-21.

36. *Collected Works*, vol. 2, p. 265.

37. Ibid., vol. 2, p. 266.

38. Martin Diamond, Winston Mills Fisk, and Herbert Garfinkel, *The Democratic Republic*, 2nd ed. (Chicago: Rand McNally, 1971), pp. 6-7.

39. James Madison, Alexander Hamilton, and John Jay, *The Federalist*, ed. Jacob E. Cooke (Middletown, Conn.: Wesleyan University Press, 1961), no. 35, p. 220.

40. *Collected Works*, vol. 1, p. 272.

41. Ibid., vol. 1, pp. 272-73.

42. Ibid., vol. 1, p. 273.

43. Ibid., vol. 1, p. 278.
44. Ibid., vol. 1, p. 274.
45. Ibid.
46. Ibid., vol. 1, p. 275.
47. Ibid.
48. Ibid.

Chapter IV

1. Lord Curzon, "Modern Parliamentary Eloquence," quoted in William E. Barton, President Lincoln, 2 vols. (Indianapolis: Bobbs-Merrill, 1953), vol. 1, p. 129.

2. Louis A. Warren, Lincoln's Gettysburg Address (Fort Wayne, Indiana: Lincoln National Life Foundation, 1964), pp. 174-75.

3. Federalist no. 1.

4. Lane Cooper, introduction to The Rhetoric of Aristotle (New York, London: Appleton-Century, 1932), pp. xxxiii-xxxiv.

5. This sort of literary archaeology is based on the assumption that writing a masterpiece is analogous to robbing a grave. The most recent in a long series of attempts to explain Lincoln's thought by what he read is Byran D. Murray, "Lincoln Speaks," Contemporary Review 208 (May 1966): 250-61.

6. See, for example, the detachment that Woodrow Wilson expresses in the introduction to Congressional Government. Wilson considers himself to have escaped reverence for the Constitution. This enables him to see how the Constitution has degenerated in practice from the noble instrument intended by the Founders. In other words, while Wilson criticizes our institutions, he does not criticize the Founders' intentions. In this his detachment is less radical than that of Lincoln.

7. Florence Jeanne Goodman, "Pericles at Gettysburg," The Midwest Quarterly 6 (Spring 1965): 317-36; William J. Wolf, The Almost Chosen People (Garden City, New York: Doubleday, 1959).

8. Goodman, p. 321.

9. Ibid., p. 322. The words "under God" are not found in the manuscripts which were written before delivery. They first appear in newspaper accounts which read ". . . this nation shall, under God, have a new birth. . . ." In copying the speech later, Lincoln changed this to ". . . this nation, under God, shall have. . . ."

10. Wolf, p. 170.
11. Ibid., p. 169.
12. Ibid., p. 170.
13. Ibid., p. 171.

14. Everett's speech may be found in Warren, pp. 185-214. The judgment which Everett quotes is that "the whole earth is the sepulchre of illustrious men." He corrects this judgment: "All time, he might have added, is the millennium of their glory." But Everett does not see the need of adding, either here or elsewhere, that they shall be rewarded in heaven.

15. Goodman, p. 328.

16. All of the extant drafts of the Gettysburg Address contain three paragraphs. However, the earliest of these has the third section in the second paragraph instead of the third. In dividing the speech where he does Lincoln perhaps wishes to point

out that the time sequence is less important than the intimate relation between the inadequacy of the cemetery dedication and the more adequate dedication needed.

17. Joseph H. Barrett, *Abraham Lincoln and His Presidency* (Cincinatti: Moore, Wilstock, & Baldwin, 1904), vol. 2, p. 208.

18. St. Thomas Aquinas, *Summa Theologica* I-II, 94-2; Jaffa, *Equality*, pp. 137, 177.

19. *Collected Works*, vol. 3, p. 375.

20. See Mansfield, "Thomas Jefferson," pp. 39-40.

21. This interpretation is strengthened by the fact that Lincoln does not mean by liberty, freedom from interference. The nation was not conceived in liberty in this sense because it had to face the interference from Great Britain. Rather he means liberty in the sense in which he defined it the following April:

The shepherd drives the wolf from the sheep's throat, for which the sheep thanks the shepherd as a *liberator*, while the wolf denounces him for the same act as the destroyer of liberty, especially as the sheep was a black one. (*Collected Works*, vol. 7, p. 302.)

It is the sheep's definition that Lincoln takes to be the correct definition. Not freedom from interference but freedom from unjust interference or from injustice simply seems to be the definition. See Hans J. Morgenthau, "The Dilemmas of Freedom," *American Political Science Review*, 51 (September 1957): 714-23, and reply by Howard B. White.

22. John Dewey, *A Common Faith* (New Haven: Yale University Press, 1934), p. 87.

Chapter V

1. Hofstadter, p. 94.

2. It shows that Masters' view, discussed in chapter I, is at least half wrong. Lincoln may be a hypocrite—he may be trying to cover up these facts with what he later says (although it then seems odd that he would say them at all). However, the "Hebraic-Puritan" ideas cannot be responsible for Lincoln's alleged lack of responsibility, because Lincoln clearly sees that victory depends on the plans and actions of men.

3. St. Thomas Aquinas, *Summa Theologica*, II-II, 83-1.

4. *Collected Works*, vol. 8, p. 155.

5. Ibid., vol. 7, p. 368.

6. Notice that men's prayers presuppose that the War is a scourge.

7. *Collected Works*, vol. 8, p. 356.

8. See Current, *The Lincoln Nobody Knows*, p. 52; and Herndon, *Lincoln's Religion*, pp. 17-18.

9. Karl Lowith, *Meaning in History* (Chicago: University of Chicago Press, 1949), vol. 8, p. 199.

10. Edmund Wilson, *Patriotic Gore* (New York: Oxford University Press, 1961), p. 102.

11. Quoted in ibid., p. 103.

Chapter VI

1. Hofstadter, p. 125.
2. *Collected Works*, vol. 2, p. 116.
3. Edmund Wilson, p. 123.
4. *Collected Works*, vol. 8, p. 333.

SELECTED BIBLIOGRAPHY

This bibliography is restricted to the works of Abraham Lincoln, to the pre-eminent general studies of Lincoln and the Civil War, and to the writings about Lincoln most important for understanding his political thought.

Speeches and Writings of Lincoln

The Collected Works of Abraham Lincoln. Edited by Roy P. Basler. 9 vols. New Brunswick, New Jersey: Rutgers University Press, 1953.

The Collected Works of Abraham Lincoln: Supplement 1832-1865. Edited by Roy P. Basler. Westport, Connecticut: Greenwood Press, 1974.

Writings About Lincoln and The Civil War

Basler, Roy P., ed. *Abraham Lincoln: His Speeches and Writings*. Cleveland & New York: World Publishers, 1946.

Bellah, Robert N. "Civil Religion in America." *Daedalus* (Winter, 1967): 1-21.

Beveridge, Albert J. *Abraham Lincoln: 1809-1858*. 2 vols. Boston & New York: Houghton Mifflin, 1928.

Bradford, M. E. "Lincoln's New Frontier: A Rhetoric for Continuing Revolution." *Triumph* VI (May, 1971) no. 5: 11-13 and 21; no. 6: 15-17.

Catton, Bruce. *The Centennial History of the Civil War*. 3 vols. Garden City, New York: Doubleday, 1951.

Charnwood, Lord Godfrey Rathbone Benson. *Abraham Lincoln*. Garden City, New York: Holt, 1917.

Cooper, Lane, trans. *The Rhetoric of Aristotle*. New York: & London: Appleton-Century, 1932.

Current, Richard N. *The Lincoln Nobody Knows*. New York & London: McGraw-Hill, 1958.

———, ed. *The Political Thought of Abraham Lincoln*. Indianapolis: Bobbs-Merrill, 1967.

DeAlvarez, Leo Paul S., ed. *Abraham Lincoln, The Gettysburg Address, and American Constitutionalism*. Irving, Texas: University of Dallas, 1976.

Donald, David. *Lincoln Reconsidered*. New York: McClelland, 1947.

Fehrenbacher, Don E. *The Changing Image of Lincoln in American Historiography*. Oxford: Oxford University Press, 1968.

———. *Prelude to Greatness: Lincoln in the 1850's*. Stanford: Stanford University Press, 1962.

Geyl, Pieter. "The American Civil War and the Problem of Inevitability." *The New England Quarterly* 24 (Spring, 1951): 147-68.

Goodman, Florence Jeanne. "Pericles at Gettysburg." *The Midwest Quarterly* VI (Spring, 1965) no. 3: 317-36.

Graebner, Norman A., ed. *The Enduring Lincoln*. Urbana: Illinois: University of Illinois, 1959.

Herndon, William H., and Jesse W. Weik. *Life of Lincoln*. Edited by Paul M. Angle. New York: Fawcett, 1961.

Hofstadter, Richard. *The American Political Tradition*. New York: Knopf, 1948.

Jaffa, Harry V. *The Conditions of Freedom: Essays in Political Philosophy*. Baltimore: Johns Hopkins University Press, 1975.

————. *Crisis of the Houses Divided*. Garden City, New York: Doubleday, 1959.

————. *Equality and Liberty*. New York: Oxford University Press, 1965.

Lewis, Lloyd. *Myths after Lincoln*. New York: Harcourt, Brace & Co., 1941.

Malone, Dumas. "Jefferson and Lincoln." *Abraham Lincoln Quarterly* V (June, 1949) no. 6: 327-47.

Masters, Edgar Lee. *Lincoln the Man*. New York: Dodd-Mead & Co., 1931.

Morgenthau, Hans J. "The Dilemmas of Freedom." *American Political Science Review* 51 (September, 1957): 714-23.

Murray, Byron D. "Lincoln Speaks." *Contemporary Review* 208 (May, 1966): 250-61.

Nevins, Allan, ed. *Lincoln: A Contemporary Portrait*. Garden City, New York: Doubleday, 1962.

————. *Lincoln and the Gettysburg Address*. Urbana, Illinois: University of Illinois Press, 1964.

————. *Ordeal of the Union*. 8 vols. New York: Scribner, 1947.

————. *The Statesmanship of the Civil War*. New York: Macmillan, 1953.

Nicolay, John G. and John Hay. *Abraham Lincoln: A History*. 10 vols. New York: The Century Co., 1890.

Pargellis, Stanley. "Lincoln's Political Philosophy." *Abraham Lincoln Quarterly* III (June, 1945) no. 6: 275-90.

Pressley, Thomas J. *Americans Interpret Their Civil War*. New York: Oxford University Press, 1954.

————. "Bullets and Ballots: Lincoln and the 'Right of Revolution'." *American Historical Review* 67 (1962): 647-62.

Randall, J. G. *Lincoln, the Liberal Statesman*. New York: Dodd, Mead, & Co., 1947.

————. and Richard N. Current. *Lincoln the President*. 4 vols. New York: Dodd, Mead, & Co., 1945-55.

————. and David Donald. *The Civil War and Reconstruction*. Boston: Heath, 1961.

Rice, Charles A. T. *Reminiscences of Abraham Lincoln by Distinguished Men of His Time*. New York: North American Publishing Co., 1886.

Riddle, Donald W. *Congressman Abraham Lincoln*. Urbana, Illinois: University of Illinois, 1957.

Sandburg, Carl. *Abraham Lincoln: The Prairie Years*. 2 vols. New York: Harcourt, Brace, & Co., 1926.

————. *Abraham Lincoln: The War Years*. 4 vols. New York: Harcourt, Brace, & Co., 1939.

Schlesinger, Arthur M., Jr. "The Causes of the Civil War: A Note on Historical Sentimentalism." *Partisan Review* (October, 1949): 969-81.

Thomas, Benjamin P. *Abraham Lincoln*. New York: Knopf, 1952.

Trueblood, Elton. *Abraham Lincoln: Theologian of American Anguish*. New York, Evanston, San Francisco & London: Harper & Row, 1973.

Warren, Louis A. *Lincoln's Gettysburg Address*. Fort Wayne, Indiana: Lincoln National Life Foundation, 1964.

Warren, Robert Penn. *The Legacy of the Civil War*. New York: Vintage Books, 1961.

White, Howard B. "Comment on Morgenthau's Dilemmas of Freedom." *American Political Science Review* 51 (September, 1957): 724-30.

Williams, T. Harry. "Abraham Lincoln—Principle and Pragmatism in Politics: A Review Article." *Mississippi Valley Historical Review* 40 (1953): 89-106.

Wolf, William J. *The Almost Chosen People*. Garden City, New York: Doubleday, 1959.

INDEX

Abington School District v. Schempp, 4, 7-10, 120, 121
Abolitionists, 22, 52, 61
Abraham, 68
Alexander, 29
Ambition, 29-31
Angle, Paul, 16
Aristocracy (and aristocrats), 31, 38, 55, 56, 58, 60, 75, 119
Aristotle, 122, 123
Articles of Confederation, the, 81
Atheism, 7-10, 12, 16-17
Athenian democracy, 44
Axioms, political, 72-78, 113

Bailyn, Bernard, xi
Barrett, Joseph H., 125
Barton, William E., 124
Basler, Roy P., 121
Beard, Charles, x
Bellah, Robert N., 120, 121
Beveridge, Albert J., 122
Bible, the, 4, 7, 9, 11, 12, 15, 35, 36, 53, 66, 67, 69, 82, 89, 95-98, 103, 121
  reading in schools, 4-10
Bill for Establishing Religious Freedom, 3

Caesar, 29, 30, 31
Calvanism, 16; *see also* Puritanism
Charity, 15, 93, 106-108
Charnwood, Lord, 10, 12, 121, 122
Chosen people, God's, 42-44, 62
Christianity, 3, 12, 23, 25, 36, 67-70
Churchill, Winston, 38
Civil War, the American, ix, 11, 15, 16, 20, 42, 43, 61, 63, 64, 68, 70, 74, 83, 88-89, 90-95, 98-106, 109-112, 115

Complacency, 23-25, 36-37
Consent, 39, 61, 75, 113-115
Conservatism, 33-35
Constitution, U.S., ix, x, 1, 2, 4-10, 30, 31, 34, 37, 81, 82
Cooke, Jacob E., 123
Cooper, Lane, 124
Corruption, 1, 15-17
Cox, Richard, vii
Criminals, 105
Critical spirit, ix-xi
Current, Richard, 15, 16, 17, 121, 125
Curzon, Lord, 64, 124

Davis, Jefferson, 90
Declaration of Independence, x, xi, xii, 3, 32, 34, 45, 46, 47, 49, 51, 52, 54, 61, 64, 71-79, 81, 82, 87, 103, 112, 113, 114, 117
Deeds, and speech, 84-86
Democracy, 2, 56, 59-60, 116-117
  defined, 44-45
  Lincoln's support of, 38-62, 54-55, 86-87
  and slavery, 44-45
Dewey, John, 82-83
Diamond, Martin, 123
Douglas, Stephen A., 43, 45, 46, 47, 49, 50, 54, 102
Douglas, Justice William O., 5-6, 10
Dred Scott, 102

Education and religion, 4-10
Edwards, Jonathan, 16
Eidelberg, Paul, 120
Engel v. Vitale, 7
Equality, 21, 38-62, 97, 106, 113-15, 116

Euclid, 68, 73
Everett, Edward, 68
Everett, William, 124
Experiment, U.S. as an, 30-31

Fame, 29-31, 67, 85
Federalist Papers, x, 56, 64, 119, 123, 124
First Amendment, the, 1, 4-10
First Inaugural Address, the, 42-44, 91
Fisk, Winston Mills, 123
Fitzpatrick, John C., 120
Founders, ix, x, 2, 3, 7, 30, 32, 33, 34, 35, 36, 49, 54, 63, 64, 71, 78, 79, 80-84, 87, 109, 113, 116
Fourteenth Amendment, the, 7
Fourth of July, 50-51
Freedom, 1, 18, 21, 44-54, 78-79, 86, 125
of religion, 4-10
Friendship, 58-59
Frisch, Morton J., 120

Gamblers, 26-27
Garfinkel, Herbert, 123
George III, 54-72
Gettysburg Address, the, 10, 11, 12, 17, 18, 19, 20, 21, 32, 36, 54, 63-87, 107, 109-119
Gettysburg cemetery, 17, 70
Goldberg, Justice Arthur, J., 9
Goodman, Florence Jeanne, 67-70, 85, 124
Grant, General Ullyses S., 90
Great men, xii, 29-31, 35, 38-42, 117, 122

Hamilton, Alexander, 3, 64, 123
Harlan, Justice John Marshall, 9
Herndon, William, xii, 12, 14, 16, 121, 125
History, 70-72, 79-83, 98, 110
Historical determinism, 16, 92, 101-104
Hofstadter, Richard, 48, 91, 111, 123, 125, 126
Honesty, 38
Honor, 29-31

Howe, Mark De Wolfe, 120
Humanism, 66-70

Ideology, 118
Immortality, 86-94
Israel, 115

Jaffa, Harry V., 42, 54, 122, 123
Jay, John, 123
Jefferson, Thomas, x, 2, 3, 4, 60, 62, 71, 72, 73, 74, 75, 77, 119, 120
Jerusalem, 68
Job, 68
Judgment, 94-98
Last, 35-36
Justice, and mob law, 23-28
passion for, 23, 37
popular sense of, 47-54

Law, obedience to, 20-37
reverence for, 20-37, 39, 124
Lee, Robert E., 90
Liberalism, 1-2, 16-17
Liberty, 1, 18, 21, 44-54, 78-79, 86, 125
Limits of politics, 87, 88-108, 110-111, 116-117
Locke, John, 1, 120
Longfellow, Henry Wadsworth, 64
Lovejoy, Elijah, 22
Lowith, Karl, 125
Lyceum Speech, the, 21-37, 38, 44, 52, 53, 54, 64, 116

Madison, James, x, 3, 123
Man of the people, 38-42
Masters, Edgar Lee, 15, 16, 17, 121, 125
Mansfield, Harvey C., Jr., vii, 120, 125
McCullum v. Board of Education, 5
McIntosh, 26
McMurtrie, Douglas C., 121
Mill, John Stuart, 121
Miller, Perry, xi
Mission, America's, 65, 109
Mob spirit, xiii, 22-23, 25-28
Moderation, 29, 106-107, 118
Montesquieu, 122

Morality, popular, 47-54, 60-62, 80, 116,
    and religion, 3-4, 15-17, 93, 121
Morgenthau, Hans J., 125
Murray, Byron, D., 124

Naknikian, George, 121
Napoleon, 29, 53
Nevins, Allan, 121
New England school of history, xi, 120
Niebuhr, Reinhold, 121
North, the, 11, 13, 18, 22, 42, 43, 46,
    88-89, 90, 92, 93, 94, 95, 97, 98,
    102, 106, 111, 112, 113, 114
Notes on the State of Virginia, 3
Novelty, desire for, 30-31, 116

Passion, 3, 28, 32, 36-37, 56-58, 65, 107
Partisanship, 17-18
Patriotism, 83
People, the, 31-32, 38-39, 44, 119
Perfection, 59-60, 116, 118
Pericles' *Funeral Oration,* 67-69
Perpetuation, of political institutions, 20-
    37, 64, 75-78, 115-117
Persuasion, 3, 17, 56-57
Piety, 94-98
Plato, 44, 123
Political scientists, 122
Prayer, 94-98, 101
    in schools, 4-10
Principles, political, xii, 16, 18-19, 20,
    60-62, 64-65, 70-78, 79-80, 84, 107-
    108, 109-113, 117
Progressive historians, ix
Propositions, political, 72-78, 80, 107,
    113
Providence, 16, 25, 89, 92, 98-104, 111
Prudence, xiii, 56-59, 61-62, 118
Public good, 10
Public opinion, 48-52, 61-62, 77, 81,
    104-106
Punishment, 13, 103-106, 114
Puritanism, 16, 67, 125
Puritans, 81
Purity, 58-59

Radical Republicans, 18
Randall, J. G., 15, 121
Reason, 21, 28, 36-37, 58
Reform, ix, 33, 37, 56-60, 65, 101, 105
Religion, in American statesmen, 2-4, 13,
    17
    Lincoln's private, xii, 11-14
    separation from politics, 1-10
    and U.S. Constitution, 4-10
Religious people, 5-10
Revolution, American, 29, 44, 51, 64,
    81, 82
    authority of, ix-xi, 32-36
    influence of, 31-32
Rhetoric, Lincoln's, xii, 12, 17, 21, 35-36,
    40-41, 65-66, 90-93, 105, 108, 118,
    122, 124
Rights, 49-50, 55, 78-79
Robespierre, 15
Roosevelt, Franklin, 13
Ross, Dr., 53

Sambo, 53
Sandburg, Carl, 123
Secession, right of, 111-113
Second Inaugural Address, 10, 11, 12,
    13, 14, 15, 16, 17, 18, 19, 21, 36,
    42, 87, 88-108, 109-119
Secularism, 7-10
Self-determination, 111-113
Self-evident truths, 72-75
Self-government, 55, 60-62
Self-interest, 45-54
Sermon on the Mount, 64
Sherman, Charles L., 120
Sherman, General William T., 90
Sincerity, 15
Skepticism, Lincoln's, 101
Slavery, 3, 20, 43, 44-50, 61, 93-94, 98,
    104-106
South, the, 11, 13, 15, 22, 42, 43, 46, 52,
    88-89, 90, 92, 93, 94, 95, 97, 98, 102,
    103
Speech, political, x-xi, 18, 19, 20, 84-86
Statesmanship, x-xi, 38-42
Stevens, Richard G., 120

Stewart, Justice John Potter, 9
Strauss, Leo, xi
Sumner, Senator Charles, 72
Supreme Court, U.S., 2, 4-10
Sympathy, 59

Temperance, 55-60, 118
Temperance Address, 55-60, 118
Thanksgiving, 2
Thomas Aquinas, 125
Thomas, Benjamin P., 122
Thucydides, 67

Union, nature of, 50-52, 80-83, 88-90, 94, 97-98
U.S. Congress, House, 121

Veneration, of Lincoln, 38-39, 42
Virtue, aristocratic, 31, 38, 55, 56, 58, 60, 119
   democratic, 38-44, 62, 119

Warren, Louis A., 124
Washington, George, x, 3, 4, 13, 16, 29, 33, 35, 90, 120
   Farewell Address, x, 3, 16
   First Inaugural Address, 13
   Second Inaugural Address, 2
Washington Temperance Society, 55
Weed, Thurlow, 17, 19, 100
Weik, Jesse W., 121
Whig party, 23
White, Howard B., 125
Wilson, Edmund, 101-102, 115, 126
Wilson, Woodrow, ix, x, 39-42, 120, 122, 123, 124
Wolf, William J., 67-70, 124
Wood, Gordon, xi, 120

Young America, 31
Young Men's Lyceum of Springfield, 21

Zorach v. Clauson, 4-10, 120